UNLEASH THE LIONESS

Unleash the Lioness

A woman's guide to fighting off violent attack

Robin Houseman

HODDER & STOUGHTON
LONDON   SYDNEY   AUCKLAND

First published in 1993
by Hodder & Stoughton Ltd,
a division of Hodder Headline PLC

10 9 8 7 6 5 4 3 2 1

ISBN 0 340 59180 3

Typeset by SX Composing Ltd, Rayleigh, Essex.
Printed and bound in Great Britain by
Cox & Wyman Ltd, Reading, Berkshire

Hodder and Stoughton Ltd
A Division of Hodder Headline PLC
47 Bedford Square
London WC1B 3DP

Why this book could save your life

Unleash the Lioness is different from other self-defence books and courses because it is professionally designed for use by any woman regardless of her age or physical ability. Its message and techniques are deliberately simple. And they work.

Whilst most self-defence techniques can be useful, unless the moves are expertly taught and regularly practised they can do more harm than good. A badly placed blow may unbalance the defender or otherwise hand the advantage to the attacker.

Robin Houseman served with Britain's most élite military unit 22 Special Air Service Regiment between 1978 and 1984. Having discovered a severe lack of unarmed combat training in the military he took up karate at the age of twenty-three. By the age of thirty he had worked his way up to 2nd Dan black belt. During his time in the army and later as a security consultant he trained special forces groups throughout the world in unarmed combat.

As his experience and ability advanced he became increasingly concerned by the poor attempts at teaching women self-defence.

He felt that nobody was providing a realistic and practical course that would give women the ability to fight back that was truly effective. Many individuals provided poor teaching of basic martial arts in order to make a few pounds and preyed on the fear of women in general. **THERE WAS NO TRULY PROFESSIONAL ALTERNATIVE**.

Upon returning to the UK in 1990 he began teaching his own version of female fighting techniques and has now put these ideas into this short book.

Robin Houseman is married with three children and is currently running a security company in London.

To Heather, Alexander, Charlotte and Oliver

CONTENTS

ACKNOWLEDGMENTS

A book of this nature could not have been compiled without considerable assistance from many people. I am thankful to the following people who offered their time and professional expertise: Bill Bache, George Boyle, Terence Strong and Steve and in particular all those women who opened their hearts to tell of experiences that they would rather forget.

INTRODUCTION

I have often been asked, "How can you teach women self-defence? You don't know how we think or feel. Only a woman can teach this subject effectively."

I believe that the differences between men and women are often exaggerated to give strength to a particular group or argument. Differences do exist but in the context of this book they are very small. Both sexes experience pain and fear in the same way and both are capable of plumbing deep reserves of determination and courage in adversity. Much is made of men's physical strength but this is misleading. The majority of men are not much taller than the average woman, they can be slow-moving and many are not particularly strong or fit. Remember, size isn't everything! Just look at those beer bellies and slouching shoulders. Men and women are much more equally matched in a fight than is commonly supposed.

The biggest difference between men and women is in the mental programming that begins at birth. Girls aren't encouraged to strike back if they are hit or bullied. Instead they scream or shout or learn to talk themselves out of difficulties. Boys instead are told to get back outside and sort out the problem themselves. They are admired for standing up to a bully with a punch or two.

One of the most important aspects of this book is to help women to overcome their fear of fighting back. Men don't think twice about it, so why should women? It isn't something that can be learned overnight, but in adversity a lot of women discover immense energy and anger within themselves. I hope this book will help you to use this to your advantage and to always be prepared to act positively should you find yourself subjected to a violent attack.

Even if you disagree that a man can understand a woman's feelings in matters of self-defence, ask yourself who an attacker is most likely to be. And who knows his weaknesses better than his own kind? During the research for this book I've interviewed a number of men who have attacked women and as a professional soldier I was attacked several times so I know what it's like if someone is out to kill you. I've learnt how to survive and I believe I have the experience to show you how to react in a similar situation.

Recently I was asked by a friend who was aware of my past in the SAS what was the bravest thing I have ever done. He expected me to tell him about an engagement in a war in some exotic land. Instead I told him of when I was fifteen years old. I was a new recruit in the army training camp and had been there about eight weeks. I had discovered that many of the young lads were far tougher than me and I made the mistake of allowing one particularly large character to hit me without fighting back. As a result many others followed his example and I was bullied incessantly. I had no escape because I lived and worked with these boys and it was a truly dreadful time.

One day, after what were the longest months of my life, another boy decided to join the list of bullies and as he hit me I suddenly decided to retaliate and I fought back. It wasn't much of a fight as fights go, but I held my own and walked away with some dignity. This, of course, didn't completely stop the bullying, but as time passed the others realised that I would and could defend myself, the bullying subsided and my life became more comfortable. Overcoming my fear and deciding to fight back not knowing what the the result would be was the bravest thing I have ever done.

Courage is not doing something special, it's managing to overcome your fear in order to function effectively and this is what I hope UNLEASH THE LIONESS will teach you. Women need to learn to fight back if they are attacked and they need to know what to do to overcome their fear. There are thousands of techniques that can be used in fighting and I have chosen a few of the most simple and effective. Some may not suit your size or build. Some may appear too complicated (although I hope not). I have tried to keep the number of techniques to a minimum so that you can master them and remember how and when to use them.

The aim of this book is for you to read it through and have something in your head that will work for you should you be attacked. The most important factor is YOU. It is YOU who will have to fight back to survive and YOU who will have to take the advantage in a difficult situation. After reading this book I hope you will learn to do this automatically, almost naturally. Sadly you can't alter society and you can't alter men. But you can change yourself and if enough women adopt this attitude then perhaps potential attackers will start to think twice.

The techniques outlined in the book are for use in situations where you honestly believe your life is in danger and where your only option is·"fight or die". They are not games to be played and they should only be practised with dummy weapons and with extreme caution. This book does not set out to criticise or replace the good advice and training that is given by the police and other organisations that specialise in the prevention of attacks. Please be aware that there are situations where given the time or the opportunity to speak and a feasible route of escape, then these techniques will not be required.

This book is not suitable for the education of children learning self-defence.

This book has one aim and one aim only.
To give women the ability to fight back
against violent attack. And survive.
Its contents will shock. It is meant to.
Because understanding its message may make
all the difference between life and death –
Robin Houseman

Any time any place

Michael sat hidden in the shadows at the bottom of the slope. The street-light above the bus stop worried him. He should have thought of it earlier, he should have found a way of breaking it.

But it was too late now. The train would be arriving any minute and she would soon be walking up the road to the bus stop. Just as she had last Wednesday and every Wednesday before.

He had seen her standing there, when he had driven past on his way home from work. Always alone.

He had noticed her long black hair and the fine shape of her legs as she sat on the rail directly beneath the light. Waiting for her bus.

Dumb bitch, couldn't she see how easy it would be for someone to creep up behind and pull her down the slope into the trees?

God, she was just asking for it. How could anyone be so fucking thick?

He hadn't planned it, he had simply turned off the road on his way home. The fantasy of it had been simmering in his mind for days and tonight it was suddenly just something that seemed like a good idea.

Anyway, she deserved it. Bloody woman! She was just like the rest, laughing at him behind his back or sniggering at his looks.

They knew he was shy and tongue-tied and so they took advantage. They weren't *worth* speaking to! Even if he did talk to them he knew they would only laugh, so he didn't bother. Never had bothered with them, in fact.

Fucking bitches. They deserved all they got.

The sound of shoes on the pavement caught his attention. Distracted by his thoughts, he hadn't noticed the arrival of the train, but now he could hear it pulling out of the station . . . So the footsteps had to be hers.

His heart was pumping so hard he could feel his Adam's apple jumping with each beat, his breath so loud in his ears that he felt sure she must hear him. Calm down, he chided himself. You can't even see her yet . . .

Then she was there. Under the street-light, hands in the

pockets of her mid-length black coat. Briefcase on the ground beside her. A proper little madam. Who the hell did she think she was? Her back was to him, but there was no doubt it was her. That thick, shiny long hair. And, yes, she was quite alone.

"Wait a bit," he thought. "Wait for the traffic to go quiet. Make sure there's no one else around."

The Stanley knife from his tool box lay in his right hand. Just to frighten her, not to use. To make sure she kept quiet and didn't do anything stupid. Of course if she did, then it would be her fault for being so thick. If she didn't have the brains to do as she was told and keep her mouth shut, then what else could he do? The knife was only there to scare her.

Mind you, look at the way she's standing there, cocky slut. A nice cut across the nose would soon knock that out of her. Not a bad idea to put her in her place anyway. Fuck up their pretty faces and they wouldn't be so keen to laugh at him any more.

Funny though, she didn't seem bothered, standing there on her own. As if she hadn't a care in the world. You would have thought she would have had more sense, silly cow.

He was moving forward now. It was pointless listening for the traffic; all he could hear was the blood rushing in his ears. The adrenalin powered him up the slope in just a few strides.

She had begun to turn at the moment his arm went over her right shoulder. His forearm smothered her mouth as he jerked her backwards over the rail and down the slope into the dark. He lost his footing, but not his grip across her throat.

"Got you!" he thought as they rolled down to the bottom. "Got you now, you cocky bitch!" He pulled her to her feet and began dragging her towards the sanctuary of the trees.

The sudden pain in his forearm came as a surprise. He tried to yank his arm away from the teeth that were tearing at the back of his hand. He wrenched his hand free only to feel a piece of his flesh torn off and to see the knife fall from his bloody hand.

As the momentum of their struggle pulled her around, the light from the street lamp caught her eyes. They were glazed and wild. He could see the crazed anger in them. Suddenly he felt uncertainty and fear well up inside him. This wasn't supposed to happen!

Then an unbearable torrent of pain exploded as claw after claw raked down his face. Again and again. An unrelenting series of raking, gouging blows. He couldn't see, his face warm with his own blood.

He had to get away from the pain. Backing away blindly, he stumbled and fell to his knees.

She was gone, scrambling up the slope and into the light. The scream as he charged up the muddy bank after her was a frenzied mixture of pain, fear and an inability to think of anything else to do. He could only see with his left eye and, as he rose up at the top of the slope, he was not aware of the briefcase before it struck him square in the nose, sending him back to the bottom of the slope in a semi-conscious, bleeding mess.

The girl, shaking and crying with anger, fear and relief, waved frantically at the bus until it drew to a halt.

She collapsed thankfully on to the warm front seat, her breath coming in short panting sobs as she began to tell the bus conductor what had happened.

She looked down at her hands and didn't know whether to laugh or cry. She was shaking like a leaf. The nausea in the pit of her stomach was welling up at the thought of that filthy disgusting animal with his hands on her body.

Almost on the edge of hysteria, she began to sob.

Daily Express TUESDAY 12th NOVEMBER 1991
By John Twomey

Crime in London is soaring with the annual number of offences heading towards a million, it was revealed yesterday. Rapes, violent attacks, armed robberies and car thefts all showed big increases. Rapes increased by 18 per cent to 1,120, or three every day. Sex offences rose by five per cent.

Chapter One

THE SPIRAL
OF VIOLENCE

Daily Telegraph TUESDAY 5th MARCH 1991

Victims should always resist their attackers with all the
force they can muster, says a Home Office report
published yesterday into the psychology of sex offenders.
The study found that in half the cases where the attacker
used gratuitous or "excessive" violence the victim had
offered little or no resistance.

This is not a book about statistics. Nor am I going to fill these
pages with the same material that you can read every day in
your national newspaper.

Nevertheless, the statistics *are* alarming and are so common-
place that they are often not remembered. We all know that
women around the world get attacked every day. On holiday,
on the streets, even in their own homes. This book is not about
why or how many times it happens or even about what the
Home Office and the police force intend to do about it. This
book is about what *you* can do about it should it happen to you.

There is an increasing number of attacks on women. Everyday the newspapers publish the stories; governments condemn
the violent crime-wave; the police ask for more money to patrol
the towns; and the law-courts put offenders away.

So that you are aware of the risks to you, here's a brief summary
of assaults and violent attacks against women in 1992. Over
180,000 women are assaulted in Great Britain every year. Of that
number there were 22,537 sex attacks on women of which 4,142
were rape victims. The most serious figures arise in inner city
areas with London leading the list with 4,271 sex attacks during

the twelve-month period. The question of how many cases went unreported should be considered when taking these statistics into account.

From your point of view the only benefit of absorbing some of these figures is to persuade you that they are high enough for you to consider it sensible to prepare yourself for the unthinkable.

As the *Crimewatch* television programme is fond of saying: "Don't have nightmares." It will probably never happen to you. But it might and it only has to happen once.

The real message of statistics is this: *don't become one*.

Murdered in 1992/1993

Rachel Nickell, 23	Wimbledon Common. In daylight while walking dog with her small son.
Alison Mainwaring, 25	At home by gang who entered the house.
Tina Wing, 32	Finchley. Daytime when taking a walk.
Dawn Feast, 14	400 yards from her home on a golf course.
Lisa Greenway, 14	Castle Bromwich. Stabbed by other girls.
Amanda Duffy, 19	Battered in a car park in Glasgow.
Susan Healey, 20	At home in Motherwell.
Jean Keay, 62	At home in Prestwick.
Marion Henderson, 75	Street assault in Glasgow.

1st March 1993, Bournemouth, Dorset

A forty-year-old nurse was tricked away from her place of work late at night by a man claiming that he had been involved in a road accident outside the residential home in which she worked.

As she left the building he attacked her. She fought so bravely and with such determination that she was not raped.

However she suffered serious wounds to her head and face.

The police were searching for a man with obvious scratches to his face and hands.

All in a day

On 21st January 1993 I picked up the *Daily Express* and decided as an experiment to cut out all the murder/rape articles from the newspaper. The following are just the opening paragraphs:

The killer of schoolgirl Johanna Young has dumped her bloodstained jeans at the spot where she was murdered, police revealed yesterday.

Jill Seward suffered a terrifying ordeal in what came to be known as the Ealing Vicarage Rape, but tirelessly, and with great dignity, she told her story in order to give hope to other victims.

A savage sex attacker who slashed a girl's throat and tried to burn her alive was jailed for twenty years yesterday.

A butcher who claimed he comforted stabbed schoolgirl Claire Tiltman as she lay dying was arrested yesterday.

When he murdered John Lennon, Mark Chapman gained a notoriety that the world won't let him forget.

A crack-down on teenage crime was announced by John Major last night. He told television viewers the Government aimed to "stop it in its tracks before it becomes a habit".

One day in one paper and what does it say? It was happening years before, it is happening now. And the Government is going to stop it before it becomes habit-forming? Don't hold your breath.

Chapter Two

INSIDE THE MIND
OF THE ATTACKER

When I began to learn martial arts in 1983, I thought that I was pretty tough, especially since I was already serving in the SAS. As the years passed and my skills and knowledge of self-defence advanced, so did my understanding of myself and other people. It became increasingly clear that most men actually rely on rage and bluff to confront an opponent. When a fight starts, unless weapons are used, very little damage is done without a considerable amount of effort. Simply put, untrained people can't fight effectively. Violent men are usually cowards who use their size to intimidate others.

My understanding of martial arts developed along with my personal confidence until my adversaries no longer antagonised me and I rarely became involved in arguments or violence. I could defend myself and could therefore step aside without any loss of dignity. Self-confidence had replaced the short temper and rudeness that had existed before. I had changed.

I could, though, still understand and remember the feelings of inadequacy that prompted other young men to try and prove themselves. In more primitive times young men would satisfy their natural and primeval need to prove their manhood on the battlefield or in the hunt for dangerous animals. But today, without sport, the army or some other physical or mental challenge young men have no place to test themselves or to gain self-confidence.

Most aggression stems from insecurity and inadequacy in the aggressor

Most fights start because a man feels the need to prove *something*. Not only to others, but to himself. To have to admit to oneself that you gave up because you were afraid is a difficult thing for a young man to live with. Despite all the good intentions of our modern society, this is one thing that most people will not let a man live down. Even his friends will ridicule his weakness (as they tend to see it), even if they would have done the same in his place. Many women, too, will have little sympathy or respect for a man who does not stand his ground.

Why me?

All right, you may say, I can understand all this. But why should anyone attack *me*, unless it is to rob me for personal gain? I've never hurt anyone. I'm reasonably attractive and dress nicely, but not in a provocative sort of way. I love kids and I help old people across the road.

> A rapist who posed as a delivery man told his victim that she was to blame for the attack. A twenty-seven-year-old man persuaded the thirty-two-year-old housewife to open the door, punched her to the floor and put a foot in her face saying, "It's your fault, you shouldn't open the door to strangers."
>
> The man was sentenced to twenty years in prison for rape, assault and attempted murder. During the final stages of this particularly violent assault the victim asked him why he had picked on her? He replied, "Because you are pretty and I would never get a girl like you."

The motive for unprovoked physical attacks on women isn't always sexual. An attacker who molests women is merely using sex as a weapon. If a normal, well-balanced male wants to have sex he prefers to talk a woman into bed as a willing and eager partner. By contrast the potential rapist or sex killer is playing a power game. Usually inept or insecure in some way, he wants to exercise power over his victim – to prove something to himself and to force a form of fear and respect he doesn't normally get from women. It is a recurring theme in the confessions of serial killers that they are driven by a need to dominate submissive and compliant victims – male or female.

I can hear you say: "I can hardly believe that! Surely such

people must be mad." There are relatively few severely mentally ill people around. But there are plenty of seemingly ordinary folk who are mentally maladjusted. Or to put it another way in this computer age, there is something wrong with their programming.

What makes a man attack a woman?

There are many reasons why some men attack women. Psychologists and psychiatrists argue at length to establish common reasons behind this kind of behaviour. Often there are severe relationship problems or problematic family backgrounds that cause such dysfunctional behaviour. Nearly all men who attack women have difficulty in relating in a normal way with women. For the purposes of this book, however, all you need to know is that the man who is likely to attack a woman has something wrong with his programming. He is not someone you will be able to relate to as you would, say, with your brother or boyfriend and you mustn't try to do so.

This is how his programming may have gone wrong. A lot of men have a lack of understanding and fear of women. This can make them feel very insecure and vulnerable. Since the day they are born, most boys find that women control their lives. Mothers, grandmothers, aunts and sisters dominate the household, making all the rules, telling them how to behave. When it comes to adolescence, many boys become tongue-tied and hesitant and when they finally pluck up the courage to ask a girl out for a date they are often turned down. Nearly all of us – women and men – will recognise such disappointments from our youth.

Most well-adjusted young males soon realise that in life you can't win them all and they just move on – their confidence is shaken but not stirred. But consider the few who are not so rational and whose programming, for whatever reason, is not so well-balanced. Like Michael in our introduction.

What happened to him? Did it all start with something that he experienced or saw in childhood? Was it gradual? Was he turned down by a girl he idolised at school whom he had placed on a pedestal? He may have been highly sensitive and introverted and was left feeling rejected and unworthy, shrinking back into his shell. Did he then discover that same girl who had so beguiled him "doing things" with another boy behind the bike shed? Later he might have discovered that she was going out with a lad who everyone knew was the school Casanova? So perhaps he retreated further into solitude. Resentment festering . . .

As Michael grew older he saw wholesome, respectable young women pushing prams. He knew what they had been doing – they didn't get pregnant unless they were lying on their backs with their legs apart. Get the picture? Michael did – in his mind he could see them all doing it. Enjoying it with others, but still laughing at him. All around him he saw women flirting, even having affairs, but never with him. Then he realised that even his prudish mother and aunts had enjoyed sex. He felt betrayed and lost, and hid behind a veil of prudery and disapproval.

When he finally got married his wife also began to dominate him, just like his mother. Because he was so morose and introverted, and not very accomplished in bed, she gradually rejected his sexual advances. He found solace in prostitutes who would only make love to him if they were paid . . . The cycle is complete.

So when one day he sees some superior stuck-up bitch, waiting in her business clothes at a bus stop . . . That's enough.

In 1992 Dr Allen Leonard of the Psychology Unit of Wormwood Scrubs, carried out a study called *The Family Background of Serial Rapists*.

One of the most significant findings in this report was that the majority of the cases studied came from a violent family background. Almost all the rapists interviewed had a very poor relationship with their fathers.

In this report robbers were used as a control group against rapists. One significant conclusion from the report is this:

"Although both groups appear to experience similar amounts of disruption of parental care, more rapists report parental violence as a regular feature of home life."

An exceptionally insecure man can be made to feel even more insecure by women, to the point where he will be convinced that all women are laughing at him. This can build up so that he begins to resent and hate *all* women. He will be unable to communicate with women and will probably have no release for his frustrations. There will be no one to give him confidence or to soothe his crushed ego. It is a combination that can become a dangerous cocktail.

Often attackers do not plan to carry out an attack. They simply see an opportunity and exploit it, just as a youth does not necessarily plan a burglary but sees an open window and acts on impulse.

All this will give you an insight into the mind of an attacker, but there are many variations on the theme and other motives, from robbery to revenge and jealousy.

The point is not to suggest that you analyse or even feel sympathy for an attacker. Far from it. There should be enough clues in what you have just read for you to realise the potential time-bomb that could be ticking in the minds of some of the male population. They form a tiny, tiny minority but they are out there. Somewhere.

Too close for comfort . . .

Statistics of violent attack prove beyond doubt that the most likely place an attack will happen is in your own home. Most murders, too, are committed by someone close to the victim – a drunken husband, a jilted boyfriend or a jealous lover.

June 1992, Bournemouth, Dorset
Jane Harvell's body was found in her seaside flat where she had lived for only a month. A post-mortem showed that she had died from repeated blows to the head. Jane was 5'2" and twenty-six years old. She was an intelligent, educated adult who was attacked in the safety of her own home.

The minority are anonymous attackers who strike out of the night like Michael. But many will have something wrong with their mental programming, just like him, although the actual reasoning and triggers for an attack may be different.

But victims of "crimes of passion", as the French call it, can be just as violently raped, badly injured or murdered by those they know, as by those they don't. And just think how many women each year discover that they had been unwittingly married to a murderer . . .

So no analysis. No sympathy. If you are the victim of any violent attack, you are potentially fighting for YOUR LIFE.

Chapter Three

TRUE LIFE STORIES

Unfortunately, there are few statistics available about incidents where attackers have been beaten off by their intended victims. For the very reason that the assault was thwarted, it tends not to be reported.

Women usually want to put such events behind them as soon as possible; few have the appetite for a visit to their local police station. Many are ashamed that an attack has taken place and frequently will not even tell those closest to them. There are women though who have fought back and survived an attack. The following true accounts happened among people I know and each one shows how effective this form of self-defence can be. The names of the women have all been changed.

Shirley

Shirley is a nurse aged twenty-seven. Married with two children, she was born in a South Wales mining village where she grew up with her three brothers.

"My father always believed that people should stand up for themselves whether boys or girls. He taught us all how to fight when we were kids. When the boxing gloves came out, I had to take part as well.

"I wasn't troubled at school because I would stand up for myself. In fact looking back I was a bit of a bully myself, even though I'm only five feet two inches tall.

"We always used to go to the local disco on Friday nights and most of the girls our age could get in because we knew the local bouncers and sometimes went out with them. I wasn't daft though, I always went with a friend and came home with her.

"On the night of the incident I had a row with my best friend outside the club – over a boy of course! She went one way and I went the other.

"I stormed off home talking to myself all the way. I was really livid. I was just in the mood to have a go at anyone.

"I heard a voice off to the side of me and before I knew it this bloke had literally picked me up and was carrying me. I couldn't see much but I knew he was big. I felt like a baby. I started screaming and tried to hit him. It had no effect at first because I was just bashing blindly at him. I remember he kept telling me to shut up and that was the first time that I saw his face. I had one arm free, my left one and I punched him straight in the eye. Then my other hand came loose and I scratched him. I kept on hitting him and hitting him. If I could have got hold of something to hit him with I would have. I was so bloody angry.

"I'm not quite sure how it ended now, but I know he must have hit me at least once because I had a terrific bruise on my face the next day. I don't remember being hit. I suppose I was just too angry to notice it. One second I was hitting him the next I was standing on my own, out of breath looking to hit him again.

"I always thought I was tough and I suppose I am, but when I got home I was shaking like a leaf and did actually shed a few tears.

"Yes, I did report it to the police. They said that I was very lucky. If my Da hadn't taught me to fight God knows what would have happened."

Samantha

In 1980 Samantha was a twenty-one-year-old mother. She lived in a two-bedroom flat in the West Midlands. Her husband was twenty-two years old and worked as a truck driver.

Sam had never known any other man than Wayne. He had been her first boyfriend, her first lover and then her husband. Sam believed that sex was something that men did to women when they were drunk.

Wayne was very ordinary. His favourite pastimes were playing pool and drinking. He sat down in his truck all day and drank with his friends three or four nights a week. His youthful looks soon disappeared at an early age, which only made him feel insecure. He wasn't a drunk or a violent man in public. He would never seriously confront another man or start a fight. But, when he went home late at night the trouble began.

He would arrive between eleven-thirty and midnight and sit casually in front of the television and demand his dinner. The routine would then revolve around him complaining because the meal was warmed up, only to be told that if he came home when he said he would, it would have been hot.

The argument would often end in a raised hand and Sam receiving 'a few slaps' around the head. She would then sit crying on the sofa while her husband slept off the beer.

She didn't consider Wayne to be a particularly violent man and she did everything she could to keep him happy, always looking for a way to please him. She had to be doing something wrong, Sam reasoned. It had to be her fault.

One night after a particularly trying day when she was seven months pregnant Wayne arrived home in his usual state to find that his dinner hadn't even been warmed up. Sam told him he would have to wait for her to cook him something.

The argument developed quickly and Wayne punched her in the stomach.

"I don't know exactly what happened," recalled Sam. "I just decided enough was enough – he'd hurt my baby. I punched him back in the face. He just stood there looking at me. He couldn't believe it.

"I knew then that if I didn't carry it through he would hit me again. So I punched him. I don't remember where but I kept on hitting him over and over, until he ran and locked himself in the toilet. I was screaming all sorts of things at him and kicking the toilet door.

"My two-year-old began to cry and I stopped. At first I was frightened to stop in case he came out and hit me. I was shaking with fury, I didn't know that I had it in me. I went to look after the baby and then I went to bed. When I woke up in the morning he had already gone to work.

"We didn't mention it for a long time until our next argument. When his hand came up, I just stood my ground. I *knew* I could beat him, you see."

Wayne never hit her again and she gradually became a more confident and self-sufficient woman. They divorced three years later.

"I'm glad, I don't regret it. I just had to learn to stand up for myself."

Sarah

In 1990 Sarah was aged twenty-five and worked as a legal secretary in Surrey.

One day she walked down a tow path by the local canal. It was the middle of the day and she was enjoying the summer sun during her lunch break.

From a distance she had seen the man walking towards her. She had noticed nothing unusual about him. His jeans and T-shirt were unremarkable and he walked past her without making eye contact.

The first sign of trouble was when his hand locked across her mouth and she was lifted completely off the ground and dumped forcefully, face down in the long grass beside the path.

"I didn't really do anything at first. All my breath had gone out of me when I landed and I could feel this great weight on my back. His hand had left my mouth and I could feel him fumbling with my skirt, but I didn't have the breath to scream. He was on my back and telling me to keep still or he would kill me.

"I didn't do anything on purpose, except try to get up. As I did our heads clashed. The back of mine with the front of his. I felt the weight lift as he rolled over and groaned. I don't think I have ever moved so fast in all my life. I was up and away down the tow path like a shot.

"When I got to the road I thought of going to the police, but I didn't. I truly could not remember what he looked like. I wasn't hurt and his clothing as I remember it would have fitted the description of about every man in town on that day. I know I should have spoken to someone but I had to get back to work anyway. Maybe they should have been looking for a man with a black eye."

Tracy

Tracy was seventeen when the following incident took place. She had left home and was living with a friend in a bedsit in south London. She used to hang around with a group who smoked pot, did drugs and generally partied.

One night they had been invited to a friend's house where the booze was flowing and the music was loud. She had accepted a smoke from someone she didn't know and suddenly felt dizzy and sick.

"I knew as soon as I took a drag that it wasn't pot, it tasted so different. I almost puked on the spot. The guy was really good at first. He helped me into the toilet and I bent down to be sick while he rubbed my back. I felt awful.

"After I was sick I tried to get up but he was holding my neck down. He pushed my head down the bowl and flushed the chain. Then he tried to rape me. He held my head down with the seat and undid my jeans. I just felt too weak and sick to stop him at this point.

"He must have let go of the seat, because I twisted over and looked at him. He didn't stop he just kept trying to get my jeans off and then he hit me in the face. I just saw red and my strength came back. I scratched his face hard. I can remember the blood running down his face. He was on his knees and my foot came up and I kicked at his balls. He hit me again harder so I hit him back. I lifted myself up on the toilet and found myself standing up, stamping on him. His trousers were half down and his cock was out. I must have kicked it and his face a few times before I got out the door.

"Some other guys had been waiting outside and when I told them what had happened they gave him another seeing to. I didn't go to the police. I didn't know what the others had done to him and I was frightened of being charged for assault.

"I always stand up for myself against men and women, if you don't no one else will. It's surprising how much strength you have when you're angry."

At the time of the interview Tracy was thirty-eight and married to a company executive.

John

John is thirty, single and lives in south London. When he was twenty-one he was convicted of rape and sentenced to serve eight years in prison.

He had severely beaten his victim before raping and inflicting other indecent acts upon her. He served six years of his sentence. He had a history of petty crime including theft, receiving stolen goods and criminal damage, although he had not previously been convicted of a violent crime.

John agreed to be interviewed provided that his name was changed.

He said he was still trying to get a job after getting out of prison and having a record didn't help.

I wanted to find out what went on inside his head before, during and after the rape and I let him tell his own story.

"I was just hanging around as usual. I think it was a Friday because I remember lots of people going out to the pub. I didn't have any money, not even enough for a pint. Most of my mates had gone up town in a car and left me behind. So I was just hanging around the street. My girlfriend was at home with some of her mates who got on my nerves, so I didn't want to go there. I ended up sitting on a park bench at about closing time; I suppose I was pretty fed up. I had nothing to do.

"Anyway this girl walked past on one of the paths and I said something like hello or something like that. She just ignored me like I was a piece of shit or something. So I went up to her and asked her who she thought she was. She didn't say anything so I grabbed her arm."

Why did you grab her?

"I don't know what I grabbed her for. I just wanted to stop her from ignoring me, I suppose. I was angry but not really with her, I suppose it was because I didn't have any money, I don't know.

"Anyway she pulled away and I held on. She started to scream. Well, I just got scared, you know, and I put my hand over her mouth to shut her up. I didn't want to get banged up for just touching her. I only wanted her to stop making a noise and I would have let her go, but every time I moved my hand she tried to scream."

Didn't you think about just running away?

"Yeah well maybe, but if she was screaming and I was running someone would have stopped me or something."

So if she had shut up you wouldn't have been angry any more?

"I don't know. I mean I wasn't that angry then but she wouldn't shut up so I hit her and she went down. I got worried then, I thought perhaps I had gone too far. She wasn't screaming any more, just crying so I grabbed her under the arms and picked her up and pushed her into some trees at the back."

Why did you do that?

"Well, I wanted to make sure she was alright but without anyone else coming along that she could scream at."

You didn't think of raping her?

"No. It never entered my head. But before I could say anything she was struggling and pulling and she wouldn't listen to me, not one word. Eventually I just cracked and hit her."

What did you hit her for?

"I just wanted her to listen to me. I got angry she wouldn't listen so I belted her."

How many times?

"I don't know. Quite a lot and that's when I did it."

That's when you decided to rape her?

"Well, I didn't like decide to just rape her, it wasn't like a decision. I just did. I just pulled her clothes up and started. She let me anyway. I mean she didn't try to stop me."

Wasn't that because you had hit her and she was frightened?

"Well yeah, but I wasn't thinking about that."

What were you thinking about?

"Well, nothing really, I was just doing it and she was letting me. The more she let me do the more I wanted to do."

Didn't you feel sorry for her?

"Well, I do now, but I had gone too far then, so I just kept on."

Did you enjoy it?

"I don't know, sort of. It was like I could do anything I wanted for once and no one could stop me. So I sort of took my chance, if you know what I mean."

Did you think of her feelings at all?

"Well, you don't, do you, not at the time. I mean I was just pissed off, you know. I felt sorry and that after, but I suppose if you want the truth the answer is no not really."

What made you stop?

"Well, I finished, you know."

How did you feel then?

"Well, she was crying and curled up and I wanted to help her, but I couldn't think of anything to do, so I just got out of it."

You felt guilty?

"Yeah, I felt guilty. I suppose it dawned on me what had happened then."

You hadn't thought about it before?

"No I told you (angry) I was all worked up and not thinking."

Did you think about getting caught?

"Well, not straight away. I got worried as I was walking home, you know, what if the police got me? I knew she had had a good look at me."

Did you think about going back?

"No I just left it."

Did you think about killing her?

"No never, I couldn't kill no one."

But you could beat them up and rape them?

"You don't understand, it's different. I don't know why I did it. I'm not a bully or nothing, I don't beat people up."

Do you think it could happen to you again?

"No, I had counselling, I don't get wound up about things any more and doing time for rape isn't easy, know what I mean?"

One final question, what do you think she could have done that would have stopped you?

"Well, if she had talked to me at the beginning I probably wouldn't have gone any further. You know, if she had said sorry or just been calm I don't think it would have happened."

What if she had actually hurt you?

"Well, she couldn't, you know, she was too scared to do anything."

But if she had?

"I don't know. I suppose once I got started, she would have had to have hurt me pretty bad to stop me."

Thank you.

August 1991, Sussex

Lynne Rogers was lured to her death with the offer of a job by Scott Singleton. He arranged an unusual meeting at Charing Cross Station, London, and succeeded in persuading her to travel with him in his car. He probably hoped to gain sexual favours in return for the fictitious job. She was found strangled in a lane in Sussex.

Scott Singleton was an unremarkable, seemingly normal man who lived in a fantasy world of his own creation. When he became frightened of being caught for sexual assault, he committed murder.

Chapter Four

ACCEPTING THE UNACCEPTABLE

So far we have established that there is a very real risk to your safety, wherever you are. The threat could come from within your own domestic situation or strike suddenly out of the blue – day or night, and inevitably when you least expect it.

Today's newspapers, on whichever day you happen to be reading this book, will confirm the dangers. You will find several chilling accounts.

Also we have begun to realise that there are countless reasons and triggers that can set such people off. These are so perverse that you will never understand them. So don't try to.

Never ever give the attacker your sympathy vote

Now we come to the most important part of this book: YOU. Or, more specifically, you and your mental programming.

It is my job to convince you that should you ever be unlucky enough to be the victim of a savage attack, you will unleash the lioness within you without hesitation and with a ferocity that will surprise even yourself. For between five and thirty seconds of your life you will have to fight like a cat defending her cubs – precisely because your life will depend on it.

From now on you will see no further reference to self-defence. Throw that concept out of your head NOW. Think of **fighting back** and **counter attack**.

For whatever psychological reasons, disturbed men do attack women and women need to be able to defend themselves against these people. The police are unable to prevent these assaults from happening (through no fault of their own); the Law is a poor deterrent, and members of the public are usually too frightened to intervene, even if they are in a position to do so. So women have to rely on *themselves*.

Some people will tell you that it is not good to learn or to use the techniques outlined in this book.

In response I would say that even our Government has to resort to drastic means to deal with violent terrorists. Policemen are issued with truncheons, riot gear and firearms to protect themselves and soldiers and law enforcers are trained to fight professionally and effectively to combat potential attackers. Do the authorities protect themselves and then forbid us to do the same? I think not. This book is about how to learn to fight back effectively.

Remember the following methods are not designed to get rid of the over-amorous boyfriend or pub pest. This is about dealing with a worst-case scenario. You have to imagine the worst things that can happen to you and learn how to deal with them. This means seriously imagining rape, murder or gang assaults. This isn't easy, but in your own interests it must be done. Because for whatever terrible things you can imagine happening to you, there is someone out there who is capable of doing far, far worse.

The techniques are simple to learn and to remember, but the mental attitude is much harder to assimilate. The idea of seriously damaging another human being fills most people (men as well as women) with revulsion, and rightly so. But when their lives are in danger all women should possess the ability and knowledge to fight back to survive. After reading this book I hope you won't think twice about doing so.

How many times have you looked at an obviously risky situation, such as accepting a lift home with someone you don't know too well, briefly considered the dangers and then chosen to ignore them? You probably got away with it and came away unharmed. In many cases the worst you might have had to cope with is a little unwanted fondling and you might think that no real harm was done.

So the incident is forgotten until the next time. After all, nothing happened. And gradually you start to believe it *couldn't* happen and, anyway, you managed to deal with the problem.

Most people believe nothing horrible will happen to them. We live in a cosseted protected world from the day we are born. When we got into trouble there was always someone who came along and rescued us. Our mothers told us that everything would be alright; the teacher let us off when we were naughty; the sweet-shop owner said he would call the police *next* time we pinched that tempting chocolate bar on the front of the counter. On television there was always a guy in a white hat to come to the rescue when the heroine was in dire straits. We grow up without seeing death or the effects of violence on the human body and virtually deny to ourselves that such horrors exist.

How many times in the cinema have you seen a man get clubbed over the head with a bottle and knocked unconscious only to wake up hours later unharmed? Of course, the stunt-men used sugar glass. In the real world the dividing line between being unconscious and death is a hair's breadth. A person is unconscious because there is brain damage. If he is out for more than a few seconds the hospitals take it very seriously indeed.

If more young men understood the dangers of kicking a man in the head, then many would be less inclined to do so.

A knife used with real intent is more dangerous than a gun; it rips and tears and remains in place long after a bullet has passed through.

Have you ever seen a dead person? We hide death in our society and do our best to pretend it doesn't exist. It scares us. It's like putting your head under the blankets at night when you hear a noise.

But one day reality comes along and slaps you in the face. It says, "You're on your own now, there's no one to help you and there's nowhere to run."

February 1993, Preston, Lancashire
A woman found murdered had her body set alight in an attempt to conceal her identity.

Police believed the killer strangled his victim, aged about twenty-eight, before taking her body to an alleyway and dousing it in petrol or paint stripper.

You still don't believe it, you haven't done anything wrong. The man lurching out of the shadows doesn't really mean it; no one could do that! It isn't really happening, it's going to be alright. He'll stop soon, he couldn't really kill me. If you survive, it becomes why me? What did I do wrong? It isn't fair.

But LIFE ISN'T FAIR. The bad guys don't always lose in the end and if you turn the other cheek it sometimes gets slashed with a razor blade.

Do you remember the bully who punched you and pinched your sweets, and then lied to the teacher when the evidence was eaten and got away with it? Today that bully has grown up. There are people who will cut your baby's face for the contents of your purse.

It isn't any good saying, "I should be able to walk on my own at night." We should be able to live our lives without confrontation, but the fact is we can't. People who do bad things are sometimes sick, but society is forgetting the well-proven historical fact that some people are just plain bad, and they like it that way. Evil people do exist. We have to remember that there are men out there who enjoy attacking women.

Facing reality and accepting the truth about life is the first step in preparing yourself to face danger. Unless you accept that being attacked *can* really happen to you and you decide to prepare for it, you may just be a victim in future statistics. When soldiers are trained by their governments, a great deal of effort and money goes into teaching them. They are given thorough training with good weapons and good equipment, but nobody can guarantee that it will be enough in every situation. Sometimes soldiers die in spite of all their training.

The same applies here. You can attend courses, or learn from this book and practise the techniques, but I cannot guarantee an always successful result. **What I can promise you, is that you will be as well prepared as is possible for any individual woman alone without a gun** and you will know that you did what you could in a life-threatening situation. Every woman who learns to fight back will be a deterrent to future attacks against women.

The last mistake you could ever make

I have no doubt that you have considered this point before.

If faced with a violent assault – particularly if your attacker carries a knife – you have wondered whether or not it would be best to just let him do what he wants to and hope he'll let you go.

You hopefully enjoy a happy and healthy sex life with your partner. You rationalise that you'd find it easier to cope with emotional scars than any physical ones. That seems to make sense. But remember this. Any man who can attack a woman with violence isn't like your gentle loving boyfriend or husband.

As I explained in Chapter 2, your attacker isn't in it for sex. He's doing this to hurt and to humiliate you and to satisfy something in his brain – a brain that isn't functioning normally.

Using the techniques in this book will almost certainly allow you to escape from most situations. Research on violent crimes in the United States shows that a woman who fights back has *three times* as much chance of escaping serious injury compared with those who do nothing.

If your assailant carries a knife, it actually becomes even more imperative to counter-attack even at the risk of being cut in the process. Because, if your attacker isn't primarily interested in sex, and he's managed to assault or rape you he's got no incentive to let you go after he has ejaculated. In fact all that is left with sex removed is the primary emotion: HATE!

As likely, if it is his first assault, he will panic. A recognised indication of this is often a body that is discovered with multiple stab wounds and lacerations. If he has done it before his motive for killing you may simply be the fear of being identified.

March 1992, Bagshot, Surrey
Mrs Manzula Almani, an attractive forty-three-year-old Asian divorcee who had come home from Kenya in 1986 to start a new life, was brutally murdered on a railway footpath. She suffered knife wounds to her cheeks, her chest, her back and her arms. There was also a cut from the left side of her windpipe to her ear. Death resulted from loss of blood.

If he is ruthless enough to attack and rape a woman, how much further does he have to go to commit murder? Many criminals would say murder is, in fact, a step back in comparison, not a step forward.

Do you really want to take that chance?

Chapter Five

REPROGRAMMING YOURSELF

Quite clearly it is always best to avoid any confrontation rather than find yourself having to fight your way out of a dangerous situation.

Apart from taking obvious precautions and avoiding risky locations whenever possible (see Chapter 8) you can often deter an attack by using your body language.

Think big, walk tall . . .

Most of us have heard of this but few actually understand how body language works.

It is often remarked that some people are "born targets". By contrast many martial artists, athletes and boxers will comment that they never seem to encounter aggression from others wherever they go. Why is this? It is certainly not because they advertise their abilities, they don't. And it is not because they are big, in fact most are quite the opposite. It is because of their body language – they don't *look* vulnerable.

If there were good karate teachers standing in a line of similar-looking people you would be able to pick them out quite easily, although you may not be able to say why. This is their body language telling you that they are confident in their ability to protect themselves.

Body language is the unconscious physical message given by you in response to certain stimuli. It is not something you can consciously control because these signals show what you are thinking or feeling inside.

Of course we can make a start by walking in a confident manner when out on the streets. But if you are operating negatively inside, it will fool no one. Dogs can read fear very easily and so can people.

To effectively change your body language, you must alter the way you *feel* in response to fear. For example, by learning some truly effective and simple ways of defending yourself, you will begin to be prepared to deal with a frightening situation.

If you imagine how you will deal with an attack situation before it happens, you will have practised what to do and will know how to react in that situation. So if you are alone on a dark street and someone is closing up from behind, instead of the fear stimulus causing you to panic, run or to think "Oh God, what shall I do?", you will be thinking "If that bastard grabs me, I'll tear his head off!"

Because you will be thinking differently, your body language will change and your potential attacker will be aware of this. He may not be consciously aware of what is wrong but he will get an uncomfortable *feeling* that something isn't right, a *hunch*. This could well cause him to back off and choose another target. Your mental strength will have reduced your chances of being attacked. So by learning how to develop your body language you will be better equipped to deal with a potentially threatening situation.

But first you must learn the techniques so that you have the confidence to fight back and can begin to develop your body language.

Doing what comes unnaturally . . .

We are all programmed to react in a certain way to certain situations and we expect others to react accordingly.

But why do women tend to scream or become hysterical in a frightening situation? It is mainly because this is what is expected of them from the conditioning they have received from the movies, television and story books. Of course there is the natural cry for help, but in general a scream of alarm is what is expected.

A man is the same, his programming tells him that big is strong and small is weak. Women are small, I am big – therefore I am stronger than a woman. His programming will also tell him that in a frightening situation women become weak and submissive, and if they don't his superior strength will allow him to beat them until they do. Simple, but to him logical.

When a police dog is trained to attack it rarely loses or gets hurt. The dog is programmed to believe it cannot lose and so it obeys its handler's command to attack with maximum confidence. Should, however, the victim play the game according to different rules, the dog will become very confused and its programming will be altered. If, for example, the intended victim turns and fights back, hurting the dog badly, the animal will become perplexed and frightened and may no longer be able to function effectively. The person being attacked may still get bitten, but with nothing to lose, knowing that he can't get away and with confidence in his knowledge of the dog's weakness, he may well succeed and escape.

Imagine you are at a friend's house and she shows you a box of little fluffy kittens. You immediately think "Oh, how lovely" and reach down to pick up a little ball of fur.

You feel secure in your position as the big human protecting the small creature. You believe the kitten won't hurt you because it is so small and weak. Suddenly four little claws and one tiny set of teeth proceed to try to tear your hand to ribbons. What is your reaction? Yes. To get rid of it as quickly as possible and to take care of your damaged hand.

This is exactly the reaction I intend to create in the man who attacks the "small and helpless" woman. I want you to suddenly become a violent she-cat, with the knowledge and ability to know exactly what you are doing. **Your purpose is to upset your attacker's programming.** You may have failed at the body language stage, but if he still attacks, the surprise of being immediately attacked back with vicious intent will confuse him. It's just not *supposed* to happen! His first reaction may be to continue, but as he begins to realise that he is being hurt and being beaten his main concern will be for his own physical safety. He will retreat – if he is still able to do so.

Fear kills the mind . . .

When a man attacks a woman he is using surprise and your fear to create confusion and terror inside you. He knows that it will cause panic and prevent your mind from functioning.

Fear literally freezes the mind, unless you know how to deal with it. To prevent this from happening you must breathe deeply for energy and strength and evaluate the situation. Should you escape? Should you scream? What is he doing? Are there more of them? What is he wearing? Where is he vulnerable? Do I have a weapon? Can I get help? Is there somewhere I can run to?

26th October 1992

A Salvation Army officer in her forties was ambushed as she walked home from church at 10.30 p.m. She was grabbed from behind with a hand across her mouth and forced into an alley-way twenty yards away and then a similar distance to a deserted area where she was raped after being threatened with violence.

Although she was fit and confident, fear, surprise and lack of self-defence knowledge meant that she was unable to prevent herself being moved forty yards, a considerable distance.

Start to think. This will again change your body language and start to disturb his plans. Your cool reaction will begin to switch the fear over to his mind and you can seize the initiative. By unsettling his preconceived notions about how you will behave you are giving him doubts about his ability to succeed.

Feeling pain is part of our programming. It is a warning to the body that it is being damaged, but it is not something in itself that will prevent the body from functioning. If you believe that a hot knife is about to touch your body and someone uses an ice cube instead, you will experience a burning sensation. That is until the actual information reaches your brain and tells you what is really happening.

Many people think that being hit causes great pain. In fact initially it only causes some discomfort and disorientation; the pain comes later. If your programming tells you that something should hurt and that you are likely to fall over, you probably will. Although this will not necessarily be as a result of the blow. Because we very rarely get hit, **the fear of pain actually creates the effect that we anticipate.**

If you believe in yourself and ignore the pain you can fight with surprising confidence and power. Imagine the effect of a man hitting you hard across the face, only to see your eyes focus in a calm hatred as you start to attack back. That's not in his programming, is it?

Go for it . . .

Many karate students learn their craft from a very young age. They become very good in their techniques and at competitions. But if their teacher fails to allow them to take the occasional knock or to confront someone larger than themselves, then fear of the unknown may well prevent them from using their ability in a real fight.

A woman who finds herself in a situation where her life is under threat (which is any continuous physical attack, because no person can predict at which point an assault will stop) must understand the consequences of not fighting back.

If you survive the attack, then rape or serious injury have their own ugly consequences, and not only for the victim. The emotional fall-out can lead to suicides, broken marriages and destroyed families. In many instances those closest to the victim can suffer horribly and unpredictably. If you were attacked and fought back you will know that you did what you could in a threatening and violent situation. This in itself will help you to recover from the ordeal. If you know that you did nothing to fight back, you will probably always feel guilty and wonder how things might have been different if you had at least tried to do something against your attacker.

Most importantly, you must not convince yourself that this will never happen to you; it can. You have to believe that you have *nothing* to lose by fighting, and *everything* to gain by fighting back. There will be nobody to help you in such situations. If someone does, it's a bonus, but you must not expect it.

You must make your decision and act on it. There will be no going back because there will be nowhere to go. When you are attacked, you must decide to fight and win. Make your aim an obsession and let nothing short of unconsciousness prevent you from achieving your goal.

When I was a young Paratrooper facing a parachute drop, I was always frightened during the approach to the jump. I learned to control my fear when it became bad by throwing what I called my "insanity switch". This was, in fact, a deliberate change of mental attitude from "What if?" to "What the hell!"

By having a clear understanding of the chances of something going seriously wrong and by accepting the small chance of a mishap I could readily carry on. We were taught that "Knowledge Dispels Fear". The only way I could function effectively was by understanding the risks involved and accepting that I had to deal with the situation.

On another occasion when slightly older, I was climbing with a friend in North Wales. As a result of bad climbing technique, I became stuck and was unable to find the next hold up. I was also unable to step down to the previous hold. And it was a long way down . . .

If I stayed where I was I knew I would soon cramp up and fall . . . So logic told me that the only option was to lunge up and hope that I could find the next hold before I fell. Oh, how I wanted my fairy godmother to appear and say it was all a dream! But no, this was real. My friend wasn't in a position to help me and I had to go for it *because I had nothing to lose;* I was going to fall and probably die anyway. So I did what I had to do and succeeded in completing the climb.

Likewise, when faced with a dangerous man you can conquer your fear by believing that you will and must succeed and that you will be three times less likely to be a victim if you fight back. You must accept that the worst will probably happen if you do nothing. Just balance the worse scenario of **doing nothing** against the worst scenario of *fighting back* and you will know that you've got nothing to lose.

The Beast Within

Like it or not the animal is in all of us, sometimes deeply suppressed and sometimes just simmering beneath the surface.

Different occurrences can activate it with surprising ease: jealousy, PMT, a constant noise and, of course, when faced with a violent attack.

For some reason many women are capable of bravely defending a child or a friend yet they have the greatest difficulty in fighting back to save themselves. As we've discussed, you may believe you can't be attacked because you've never done anything wrong.

April 1992, Catford, South London

A man with previous convictions pushed his way into a care assistant's home, he took her money and then demanded sex. He tore open her clothes and then sexually assaulted her. When he licked her face she bit his tongue. His screaming alerted the care assistant's twenty-eight-year-old son, who called the police. The attacker was sentenced to nine years. He told police officers: "I chose her because she is a woman. They are soft and can't struggle." In this case he couldn't have been more wrong.

But the greatest way of defending yourself is to believe it can happen and to think about what you would do if you were attacked. Should you be attacked you must never try to think about *why* it is happening. You will never be able to work out why or be able to relate to your attacker. He will have no guilt or remorse and he won't give a damn about what happens to you or, ultimately, your family.

Chapter Six

UNLEASH THE LIONESS

To unleash the beast within you think of someone you love. A child, a small baby, your niece or nephew. Imagine a mugger about to push a cigarette into the infant's face unless you give him all the money you have on you. So you pay up and he stubs the cigarette out in the baby's cheek and laughs in your face. (No, I haven't made it up. This has really happened.) How would you feel? What would you *want* to do if you **could**? Would your anger be furious enough to prevent such an attacker from continuing?

Dwell on those feelings for a moment and then put them aside for when you need them, where they are safe. Because that is the beast. It's there in all of us. It is a weapon, a very dangerous weapon to be taken out and used only when absolutely necessary. It is like a loaded gun. Without practice and training it can be used carelessly and dangerously to hurt everyone – including its owner. Alternatively, in the hands of a competent, trained user it can be taken out at will, used effectively and then put safely away for another day.

To know how to control this instinct you must practise taking it out, using it and then putting it away. Attending martial arts classes or a good self-defence course is an excellent way of doing this.

February 1993, Brixton, London
A fourteen-year-old girl suffered a multiple rape at the hands of three older teenagers. She was threatened with a baseball bat, had her clothes cut off with a knife and her knee slashed. She was burned with cigarettes to ensure she complied with their demands and beaten to make sure she did not report the offence.

Alternatively, try to envisage a situation (maybe a particularly abhorrent crime you've just read about in the newspaper) that makes you angry and imagine how you would deal with the perpetrators. Think how you would control your anger, make it work for you, and then calm down afterwards.

This is good mental preparation for the real thing. It is like playing war games and preparing your tactics before the real fight begins.

What to do if you feel you are going to be attacked

In a dangerous situation you may not be attacked immediately. Initially you may just be intimidated with threats of violence. Perhaps held against a wall or floor, or threatened with a weapon from a distance of a few feet.

Evaluate the situation as coolly as you can. Remember he is just a man and one with a weak mind.

Establish eye-to-eye contact with him and start to let controlled anger replace your fear.

Hold his gaze all the time, let him see the strength and defiance in your eyes. The more frightened you become the more determined you should be to achieve psychological dominance.

Have you ever argued a point with someone, only to end up staring defiantly into their eyes with nothing left to say? It's called a face-off. You may have done it as a child with your father or a teacher. They may have held your gaze until they eventually achieved psychological dominance and you looked away muttering and defeated. This is exactly the battle you must win against a potential attacker.

October 1992, Wallington, Surrey
A knife-wielding man forced his way into a mother's flat, held a knife to her throat and ordered her to take her clothes off. For fifteen minutes whilst still clutching her six-month-old son she refused. The man departed leaving the victim uninjured. The detective constable in charge of the investigation praised the victim saying that "her brave defiance had stopped an even more serious assault from taking place".

Try to recall the times you've seen an actor playing the role of an evil, terrifying and utterly convincing thug . . . and then later you've seen the same actor in a sitcom or on a chat show. He's a mild-mannered charming gentleman and you can't believe it's the same man!

Well, he's achieved that transformation by drawing on his inner reserves and his knowledge of human nature. He believes himself to be the vicious character he played for the purpose of the performance, but you aren't acting. For you it's real, you have to really have those feelings. For those few, vital seconds or minutes **you must believe in yourself and in your strength and ability to win.**

Don't speak, **look! say it all with your eyes.**

Meanwhile, if you can keep out of reach, think carefully and look for an escape. Coil yourself inside like a spring waiting to be released. Think: HOW DARE YOU THREATEN ME, HOW DARE YOU FRIGHTEN ME, HOW DARE YOU, **YOU SCUMFUCK EVIL BAS-TARD!** and look for targets where you can hit him. Don't speak unless you have something positive to say. You may feel a little insane at this point, but control it and wait for your opportunity. Transfer the fear and uncertainty to him. Let him see that he's picked on the wrong woman – you're going to be no push-over!

Do not antagonise or cajole him, your silence will confuse him. And always keep your weapons hidden.

You may find the idea of keeping silent baffling or contradictory, but screaming can in fact trigger the initial attack in order to shut you up quickly.

Save your vocal chords for when you unleash your counter-attack – your verbal fury will then be sufficient to wake up the entire neighbourhood!

Sound is an excellent shock weapon. Your attacker will be programmed to expect noise, but not the screaming ferocity of a woman who isn't prepared to take any of his crap. So decide on the target you are going to go for. And when he attacks you use noise as a weapon. Scream loudly using clear words that indicate to the public what is happening, and that you want assistance. Scream "Rape!" and "Help!"

Acoustic warfare works. It has been deliberately deployed by charging armies for centuries to undermine the morale of the enemy. It is a way of firing the imagination, of enlarging the fear of the unknown. It works in the two extremes that we use. *Complete silence* gives nothing away, creating doubt. *Excessive noise* creates an image of size and power that undermines self-confidence.

So let your pent-up fury out as you go into the attack. Let rip! He is weak and it doesn't fit his plan. It will upset him and his confidence will wither and die.

So remember: if you can dominate the situation at an early stage it will be to your advantage and it may stop an attack from taking place.

- Stand your ground. Don't walk backwards, you could fall over.

- Maintain hard eye contact.

- Think: How dare you! How dare you!

- Choose a vulnerable target on his body.

- Be angry, but control your anger.

- Be ready to respond.

Targets on the body

The human body is a very powerful machine. It is designed to absorb a considerable amount of damage and survive. The bones are designed not only to support the body but to provide protection to the vital organs. The skull surrounds the brain, the ribs protect the heart and lungs, and the muscles and layers of fat cover and protect the abdomen.

A large amount of energy can be absorbed by the body without causing any serious damage (that is damage likely to disable a fully grown man). However, if the same amount of energy that would be wasted in these regions of the body is directed at chinks in a man's physical armour, then he may be disabled very effectively indeed.

So what are the most vulnerable points of the body that can be attacked simply and effectively? Remember, ideally you only want to strike once and then escape without being chased and attacked again. So we are not going to pussy-foot about. You have to disable your attacker quickly and effectively so you need to choose one of the following areas:

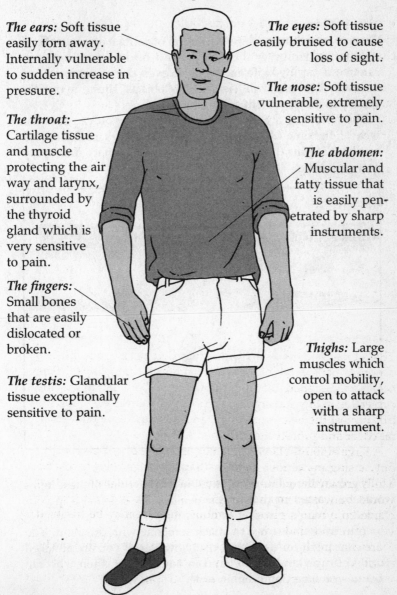

The ears: Soft tissue easily torn away. Internally vulnerable to sudden increase in pressure.

The eyes: Soft tissue easily bruised to cause loss of sight.

The nose: Soft tissue vulnerable, extremely sensitive to pain.

The throat: Cartilage tissue and muscle protecting the air way and larynx, surrounded by the thyroid gland which is very sensitive to pain.

The abdomen: Muscular and fatty tissue that is easily penetrated by sharp instruments.

The fingers: Small bones that are easily dislocated or broken.

The testis: Glandular tissue exceptionally sensitive to pain.

Thighs: Large muscles which control mobility, open to attack with a sharp instrument.

Obviously there are many other target areas, but if you strike these areas with maximum force you should be able to disarm him with one strike.

Weapons

Carrying anything with the intention of using it as a weapon is an offence. However there is a world of difference between carrying a carving knife and using an everyday object to defend yourself. The law will view such "objects" quite sympathetically in the aftermath of an attack.

The following are all everyday items that you can carry or wear all the time without breaking the law: **Keys, nail files, tail combs, hat pins** (providing you are wearing a hat), **hair spray** and **umbrellas.**

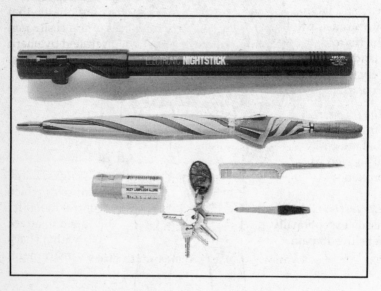

If you are in a vulnerable situation and have one of these items with you, then make it readily available by keeping it in your hand or your coat pocket *on your strongest side.*

Your intention is not to attack someone with this item. You are carrying it for its proper use; however, if you are attacked and your car keys are to hand in your pocket, then who can blame you for using them in order to survive?

Never show your improvised weapon to your attacker. You are only giving him forewarning of your greatest strength and you will lose the all-important element of shock and surprise.

If the attacker sees your weapon he can withdraw and work out an alternative attack plan. He should never be aware of the weapon until it has been used. Even after use, you should immediately conceal it in case you need to use it again on him or on another attacker who may be with him. In a dark place it is always hard to see what is happening, there may be more people than you think.

When you use a weapon, use it to its maximum effect. Drive it fully home and do not stop until your attacker is definitely disabled.

A half-hearted attack will not work, whereas a half successful whole-hearted attack will probably be enough.

A karate teacher's punch is very powerful in the classroom after years of training. But in the street – with fear, movement and an unknown enemy – he may only get it half right, but that is still usually enough to achieve the aim.

To recap:

- Be prepared and try to think ahead.

- Keep your weapon easily to hand.

- Don't show your weapon if a trouble-maker approaches.

- Don't try to frighten him with it.

- **When you use it, use it to maximum effect.**

Aggression training

When it is suggested to a woman that she should use her hands or utilise an everyday item to carry out some brutal act on another "human being", her first reaction is usually "Ugh! I couldn't possibly do that!" That reaction is exactly the reason she is vulnerable to attack.

Your attacker will have no such feeling, he will do what you hesitate to do and worse. Believe it! This is an inhibition that you must learn to overcome – albeit for only a few seconds when you are truly frightened and under attack.

Begin by learning to feel and trust your own strength. Get an interested friend and stand at arm's length from one another, placing both hands on his or her chest or shoulders and looking them straight in the eye. Okay, giggles over, now get serious.

Imagine a violent man has taken hold of you. Take a deep breath and as you shove, let all your breath out in a loud ''NO-OO!''

The act of exhaling actually gives extra power to strenuous movement. It also forces you to breathe out, many people unconsciously hold their breath when they are frightened and become dizzy or exhausted quickly.

Practise this and make a contest of it. Imagine you are pushing a car that won't start. Use the power of your legs and, as your partner goes back, follow through until he or she gives way. As you begin to experience your own strength and aggression developing, you will begin to enjoy an increase in personal confidence. Train with another female to start, but try to practise with a man as soon as you can.

Once you are feeling strong as a pusher, the next stage is to start charging and barging, combining your confidence and strength with speed and momentum. Your partner should stand with a firm pad such as a block of polystyrene about 18 inches square and about 6 inches thick (available from good martial arts stores) or some other firm material such as thick rubber or sponge held against his or her body. Stand just out of reach and charge into the pad, dropping your shoulder into the target in an attempt to knock the holder aside. It is important to stay on your feet – falling over rather defeats the object! Once the target is knocked aside continue your forward movement in order to escape.

When actually attacking exhale and use the noise weapon to increase your power and aggression. Practise the last two exercises, but as you progress concentrate a little more on letting your aggression out as you make contact with the pad. ''No!'' is a good word to use. ''How dare you!'' is certainly a good way to think.

Don't worry about the script. Say whatever you *feel*.

Now let it go.

"How dare you!"
Louder
"HOW DARE YOU!"
LOUDER!!
We all have a temper and we are all frightened of letting it loose. It's uncivilised, it's embarrassing, it's a part of you that you may not like. But remember why you are learning this. Think of the worse case. *It's necessary to practise losing your temper.*

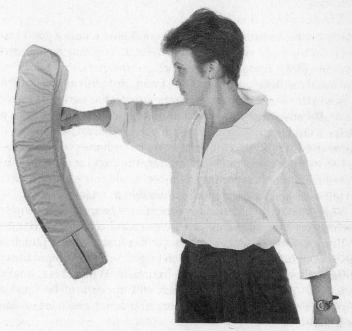

Punching an impact pad

February 1993, Southampton
A taxi driver tried to rape an eighteen-year-old girl from Buckinghamshire who was on her way to a college interview. After picking her up, he trapped her in his car using his central locking device.

He drove her to a country lane and sexually assaulted her in the back seat before she managed to kick him in the groin and escape.

Chapter Seven

TECHNIQUES WITH WEAPONS

Many people assume that because you know where a good target is on the body you will be able to hit it. You may have heard that one strike under the nose with an upward chop will drive the nasal cartilage up and into the brain. But with all the broken noses in the world, have you ever heard of it happening? I never have. Because the force, speed and accuracy required of such a strike would require years of training in martial arts. Likewise, if someone attempts to use an elbow strike with the power necessary to incapacitate a man and misses, the circular motion combined with poor positioning of the feet could cause the defender to fall over and be even more vulnerable to attack.

You will have heard of many other fancy or apparently simple techniques that, in reality, are quite complicated to carry out. When a karate student goes to his or her first lesson, a punch is just a punch. Later that one punch might combine around thirty different techniques all working in unison. When this is finally achieved to perfection the punch still appears to be "just a punch" but there may be ten years of practice and a lot of skill behind it.

The following methods avoid anything that requires hidden depths. These are **not** martial arts techniques and they do not require physical strength or skill. They are designed to be quick and effective, but to remind you once more, they are only to be used if you believe you are experiencing a life-threatening situation.

Straight as an arrow

Why is a tennis ball harder to catch when it is travelling straight towards you rather than when it is lobbed? There are two reasons.

1. It is moving with more force
2. It is coming straight at you, allowing you to see very little visible movement in order to anticipate the time of impact.

A strike with the hand or with a weapon should be the same. When moving in a straight line, there is more force behind the hand or weapon and it is much more difficult for your attacker to see it coming.

Keys

One of the most useful and handiest weapons is your set of car or house keys. When at risk they can always be carried inconspicuously in the hand. When leaving your car to visit the cashpoint or to collect a take-away meal, they offer an ideal form of protection.

Place the bunch in the palm of your hand and select the longest, most pointed key, passing it between the index and middle finger of your strongest hand. Close your fist, allowing the selected key to protrude forwards.

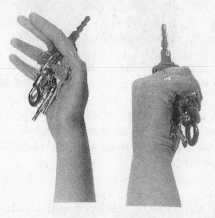

Holding your keys

Do not walk around with your keys held in this fashion unless you believe you are in danger. This can be perceived as carrying an object with the intention of using it as a weapon.

If you are approached, keep your hand down by your side, out of sight. Should an assault begin you should select a vulnerable target (see page 53) and, using a straight punching action, drive the key in to its full length.

Before deciding to strike at the body be sure that your attacker isn't wearing a thick coat or jacket as this may provide adequate protection against your counter-attack. Other available targets should be considered, such as the throat, the eyes or the upper leg.

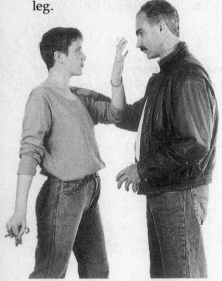

*Feed with the
empty hand*

*Strike with
the key*

Keys can be used just as effectively against an attack from the rear. They can be stabbed into or ripped across hands holding you around your waist, or downwards and back into the thighs, or backwards over the shoulder into the face.

Nail files

Try to buy nail files with small plastic handles as the all-steel versions are very difficult to use without damaging your own hand. Held and used in the same way as a key, it is another practical weapon in your armoury.

Tail combs

Buy a comb with a long thin metal handle (a tail comb). The comb should be held in the hand with the tail close to the wrist running up the arm; in this way it is invisible and ready to use against an attack from the rear. If this takes the form of a grab around the neck, the point of the handle should be brought down sharply into the attacker's groin or thigh – and pulled out immediately to be used again.

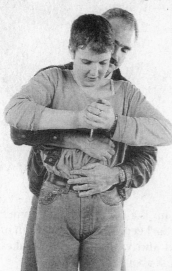

Tail comb strike to back of hands

Tail comb to upper thigh or groin

Tail comb to face

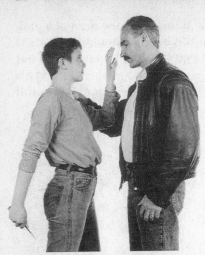

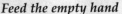

Feed the empty hand   *Strike to stomach*

With a frontal attack, simply flip the comb around in your hand so that the tail points forwards, keeping it down and out of sight. Lead with your free hand and when the attack takes place, drive the point upwards just above the belt line.

When defending yourself with a stabbing instrument **never** hold it out to the front. Keep it back against the side of your body. When it is held out it can be grabbed or avoided.

Hold out your *empty* hand as a guard. If he grabs it, you will have used up at least one of his hands and will be close enough to drive your weapon home.

Umbrellas

The long umbrella can be a useful weapon so long as it is used correctly. So forget the idea of beating someone over the head with it in the image of an old granny!

The only dangerous parts of an umbrella are its point and its handle. If you swing a long blunt weapon the effect is a weak, time-consuming swing that can be easily deflected.

Use a long, rigid umbrella like a spear. Hold it tightly in both hands, the leading hand in the middle of the length and the other on the handle. Keep the weapon held back alongside the body, ready to strike forwards as if it were a rifle with a fixed bayonet.

Always aim for the centre of the mass, either the face or the body. This allows for any unexpected movement from the attacker and any error in your aim. Strike in a straight line and pull back quickly, keeping the umbrella pointed straight at his body and ready to strike again. **Never lower your guard until the attacker has gone.**

Remember once again, do not hold the weapon out in front of you. Keep it back.

(Correct) Umbrella held back: ready position   *(Incorrect) Umbrella held out in front*

Thrust to face   *Thrust to body*

Hair sprays

Gas canisters containing riot gas or Mace are illegal in the United Kingdom, but a useful and effective substitute is one of the small cans of hair spray which are available at most supermarkets or pharmacists. About six inches long, they fit nicely into a coat pocket or the palm of the hand.

Once again this should be kept down and out of sight until the attacker has closed in on you. Feed him your empty hand and then bring up the hand holding the hair spray. Spray into the eyes and continue to saturate the area of the eyes for as long as you can. You may want to follow up with another disabling attack or to immediately escape. That sort of decision can only be made at the time.

To blind someone temporarily, it is not necessary to get both eyes. If you damage one eye the other will weep in sympathy, blurring his vision. It is also very hard to run with one eye closed.

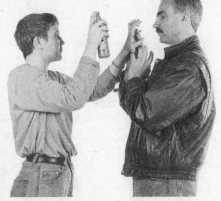

Feed empty hand and saturate eyes

Nightsticks

'NIGHTSTICK' is a portable vehicle alarm system designed to be attached to the steering wheel of a car. Made of hardened steel it is 14 inches long and can also be used as a torch. This is another device that you may have in your possession to use as a torch or vehicle alarm which can be improvised with great effect when fighting back. It is a heavy object, weighing around four pounds, and is quite capable of fracturing the skull and killing a man.

To avoid causing death and to use the object to its best effect, use the Nightstick, or any long instrument such as a heavy stick, as a prod and not a club.

It should be remembered that the only truly dangerous part of a long weapon is the end furthest away from the hands in which it is held. If the weapon is swung in a curve it takes a long time to reach the target and may allow an attacker to avoid it. And if you miss, you lose control of the weapon; it will continue to travel past your attacker allowing him to move in.

Any long weapon should be held in exactly the same way as the umbrella (in two hands) and prodded into the face of the attacker in a short, sharp, penetrating movement. By jabbing in a straight line this form of counter-attack is very difficult to see and therefore difficult to avoid. You will maintain good control of your weapon, you can recover quickly and will be able to strike again. By using the weapon in this way you are maintaining a position of defence that is hard to penetrate.

Pens

Pens can be used quite effectively as weapons although they are hard to grip when applying any leverage.

The best way to hold a pen is across the palm of the hand with the point protruding out between the thumb and forefinger. With the hand tipped forward the pen should be pushed into

Holding a pen

the eye. Or when held in a fist, it can be jammed into the ear with a sideways swing.

Used on other parts of the body it will not penetrate clothing or incapacitate sufficiently.

Defence against knives

The best defence against a sharp instrument, such as a knife, is a shield. Keep your shield between you and the attacker until he exhausts himself or until you can get assistance.

There are many types of shield. There are of course the obvious ones such as dustbin lids, but other examples include books, blankets, coats and chairs.

Hard shields should be used to directly block and deflect knife blows, whereas soft shields such as coats and blankets should be used to entangle the knife and arm of the attacker.

The best shield commonly available is a chair. Hold the seat and back of the chair at arm's length with the four legs pointing forward in a diamond shape at the attacker. Aim the top leg at the throat. The two middle legs will then point at the shoulders or upper chest and the lower leg at the abdomen or groin. Used in defence it is an ideal shield. Used in attack by rushing towards your assailant using your speed and weight it becomes a truly effective weapon. It is an excellent way of pinning a man against a wall or to the floor.

If one of these shields isn't readily available a blanket or coat can be wrapped around the leading arm with a piece dangling down. Hold the wrapped arm out, it will be protected from cuts, then try to swing the blanket or coat around the attacker's weapon. Never grab a knife in self-defence, always grab the wrist holding it. In this way you can maintain control. If you can find a long instrument such as a broom or, if you are in the country a stick, hold it up high and strike down at the wrist holding the knife. Striking the wrist hard will cause the fingers to open and the knife to be released. If all else fails accept the danger and attack the face as viciously as you can in order to blind your attacker and escape.

December 1991
Geraldine Parks' mutilated body was found in a stream the day after she took a taxi home from an office Christmas party at midnight. She had 250 yards to walk to her gate!

Chapter Eight

TECHNIQUES WITHOUT WEAPONS

Many attacks begin with a grab of some kind. Releasing yourself quickly and effectively from this situation may allow a prompt escape.

One of the most common attacks on a woman is the attack from behind with an arm across the throat. This prevents the victim from making a lot of noise and can eventually cause submission by cutting off the air supply.

Breaking a stranglehold

The natural reaction to a stranglehold is to put your head back in an attempt to relieve the pressure on your windpipe. Unfortunately this is the worst thing to do as it causes the windpipe to protrude, exposing it further.

Instead practise pushing *forward* into the arm across the throat. The large muscles on the side of your neck will bulge forward in advance of the windpipe, preventing your airway from being compressed.

This should be your immediate reaction to any attack to the throat from the front or rear. It gives you time to think, takes

Side muscles of neck protecting windpipe

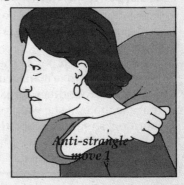

Anti-strangle move 1

away the advantage from the attacker and prepares you to deliver a counter-attack of your own.

Anti-strangle holding wrist and elbow

February 1993, Oxford

Following a row with her boyfriend, a twenty-seven-year-old pharmacist was attacked when she walked home alone.

A man grabbed her as she was walking past some railings. Although she managed to get hold of his hair, he had his hands around her throat. The woman told the court that she thought she was going to be found dead the next morning, so she conceded to his demands to save her life.

He then dragged her into an alleyway and tied her hands before raping her.

Once you have carried out the anti-strangle action, bring your hands up to the wrist and elbow of the arm across your throat, push your hips sharply back into his groin as if attempting to pull him forward over your head. Then flick your head back sharply and with maximum force so that the rear of your head makes contact with his face. When carried out correctly, this

*Head forward
Hips back*

*Back of head
strikes nose*

action should break his nose or cheekbones and disable him long enough for you to make good your escape. If you are much shorter than your attacker this technique will still work because the man will be forced to bend his body to reach your height. You will probably be surprised by how much weight you can carry on your back. Practise pulling someone over your back to convince yourself that you can do this easily. **And if that doesn't work . . .**

Remember that you were told to bring your hands up to the wrist and elbow of the arm across the throat? If your first plan doesn't come off feed your thumb between the fingers of his hand, preferably getting hold of *only* the little finger. In one sharp movement – with **MAXIMUM** force – jerk the finger backwards and downwards towards the elbow of the same arm. Done properly this will dislocate his finger at the knuckle.

*Search for the
little finger*

*Twist back and
down*

Break it!

This will cause sufficient disablement to allow you to escape.

Again, in this training programme you are reminded to do
nothing half-heartedly. Because if you bend the finger back
slowly (although this will cause your attacker severe pain), it
will become increasingly difficult to break or dislocate. He may
well wriggle out of the hold.

Once you have the advantage, use it. You may not have it again.

Alternatively you can use this technique in a different way. Carry out the anti-strangle action and flick back with the hips to create a gap between your two bodies. At the same time, form your hand (the one on his elbow) into a straight-fingered upright position. Strike down and back, allowing your hand to chop down behind your buttock, following the natural line into his groin.

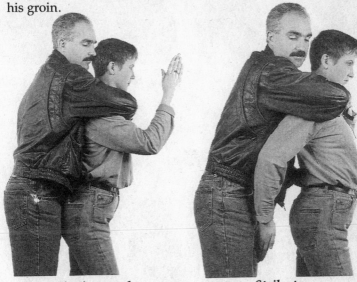

*Anti-strangle
raised chopping hand*

*Strike to
groin*

A strike in this fashion will cause him to move his hips back leaving him open for a repeat strike or to follow-up with the backward head butt or finger break as previously described.

If you are held by the throat from the *front* in the classic strangler's hold, again push *into* the hold, pushing your chin down towards the fingers and thumbs gripping your throat.

At the same time bring your thumbs up and under the attacker's little fingers (which will be the lowest) and jerk them both upwards and backwards towards his elbows. This will effectively break or dislocate them. To add power to this action, as you jerk the fingers back squeeze your elbows in towards each other so that they meet in the centre of your body (see p72).

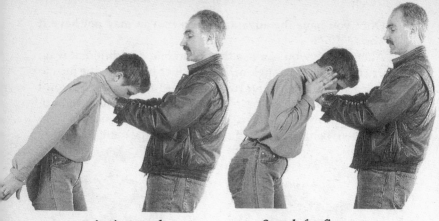

*Anti-strangle
front*

Search for fingers

*Bend back
and down*

*Squeeze elbows together
and break*

Breaking a wrist grab

If you are grabbed by the wrist the simple method of release is to jerk the wrist sharply in the direction of the attacker's thumb (upwards) on the hand that is holding you.

His thumb is operating as one side of a pincer grab on the wrist and is far weaker than the remaining fingers operating together.

Therefore this sharp sudden movement is enough on its own to release the hand from the grip. You will then have the choice to run or to follow with your counter-attack.

*Wrist hold
break by jerking
towards thumb*

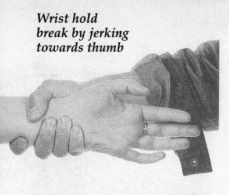

How to use your hands
Ears

Many women have the habit of striking with their fists to the side of the head. If you are in the position to do this, then simply open your hand flat and slap hard over the whole ear in a cupping action.

Done with enough force this will burst the eardrum and cause extreme pain. If this hasn't achieved the required result, then close your fingers over the whole ear, grip tightly with your fingernails and pull hard.

The ear will tear off in your hand. Drop it (as he will probably want it back) and run.

If you hold the top of your own ear as an experiment and pull gently down towards the ground you will understand how easy and effective this technique can be.

Cupping hand for ear strike

Gouging the eye

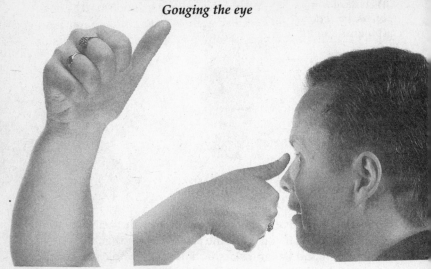

Eyes

Gouging eyes is a very effective way of disabling an attacker. Unfortunately it is also the one technique that many women find most abhorrent. Now, this far into the book, you should have convinced yourself not only that you *can* do this, but also that you *must* and *will* do it.

Do not use the infamous two-fingered karate strike as you'll probably miss and damage your fingers on his head. Instead use just your thumb and go for one eye only. The thumb is very strong and mobile. Screw it into his eye. The eyeball will not pop out or burst; it will weep, bleed, bruise, swell, and hurt like hell. And because the other eye will weep profusely as well, he will be blinded enough for you to escape or to strike at another vital point.

Clawing

Raking usually comes naturally as a female form of attack. Scratches on the face are not uncommon after a female–male conflict, but to rake effectively in a dangerous situation form your hand into a tiger's claw and, when you attack, go for the front and centre of the whole face with the fingernails striking just above the eyes. As the fingernails make contact they should rake downward, entering into the eyes if possible. Then on down across the nose and cheeks, taking as much skin as possible off the face. Follow immediately with the other hand forming a continuous rotating, climbing action with both hands on

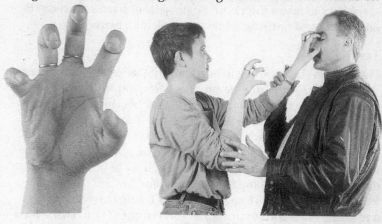

Tigers claw

*Raking the face
(above right
and right)*

the face until he collapses or retreats. Don't give up on your advantage, *attack until he can no longer attack you.*

Biting

Teeth are a great weapon. They are very strong and can cause terrible damage and pain. Targets for teeth are the soft tissues of the face, neck, chest and groin. These are the nose, ears, cheeks, the neck, nipples and the genitals.

When you bite you **must** be prepared to take a piece of flesh with you in order to disable and shock him into stopping. Bite, tear, and rip (remember he is trying to rape or kill you!).

Fingers are also good to bite, but it would take an exceptional set of jaws to take a finger off. So just bite as hard as you can to cause pain and bruising while you look for a better target.

Testicles

The groin is always going to be a favourite target to attack but of course it is also the one he most expects you to try for. Tight jeans provide considerable protection by holding the testis up and a simple turn of the knee is an effective guard against most strikes. If you can attack here of course do so, but to a man wearing tight trousers a grab is ineffective. You must strike sharply upwards by clenching your fist as if you were holding a mug handle. Then by keeping the striking hand low and feeding the free hand towards his face, swing your fist up between his legs and strike hard with your thumb uppermost. Try to strike the face with the other hand as this will continue to keep his hands high, exposing his groin. Secondly this gives you another attack in the making if the first one fails.

Feed the empty hand

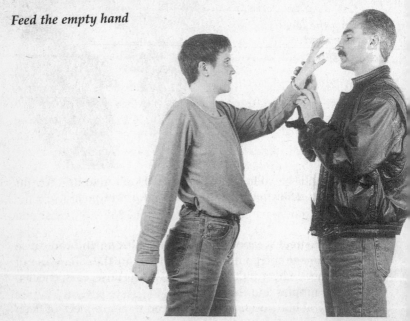

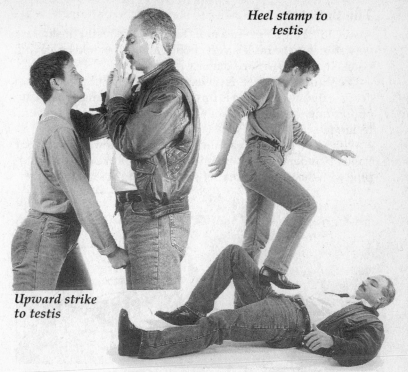

Heel stamp to testis

Upward strike to testis

If a man's genitals are exposed during an attack and you are in a position to do so grab hold of his testicles (not his penis) and try to squeeze, twist and pull at the same time. This may be lethal; they may be torn off if pulled hard enough.

Getting the victim to perform fellatio is a favourite with sex attackers. If the attacker exposes his genitals to your face he is probably convinced that he has hurt you sufficiently to obtain your complete submission.

This could be your only opportunity to save your life. Bite his penis hard until you know it is bleeding. This will force the attacker to move, so grab his testicles and squeeze, twist and pull.

Do not be too keen to pull your head away from his groin as it will be difficult for him to attack your face or stab another vulnerable part of your body while your head is between his legs.

Make sure the damage is severe enough to disable, before you release and run.

The throat

Avoid attacking a person's mouth. It is full of teeth, the lips are very stretchy, the neck is very mobile and you would be leaving yourself open to serious damage.

The throat, however, is an excellent target. But a man's chin drops naturally when he is threatened, so you must look for an opportunity and then drive into the throat with one of several techniques:

With your hand spread and palm facing down, drive your hand up under the chin and into the throat. Strike into the windpipe with the webbed area between your thumb and forefinger.

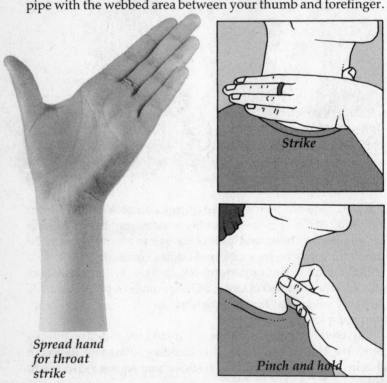

Strike

Spread hand for throat strike

Pinch and hold

Then grab the windpipe with your forefinger and thumb and pinch in behind it hard. This will cut off his air supply. No matter what he does from this point on, you will have the advantage. Keep him held until he loses consciousness and then escape. Once he collapses, follow him to the ground maintaining your grip. Hold on for another few seconds, just to be sure he isn't bluffing. Then let go, or you will definitely kill him.

Alternatively, turn your hand palm-up and bend the fingertips down to make contact with the top of the palm of the hand, to form a narrow fist (see diagram). This will slide up under the

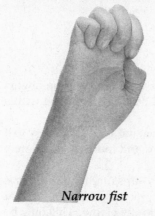

Narrow fist

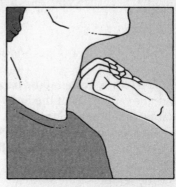

Strike upwards to larynx

attacker's chin to punch the Adam's apple (the larynx). Any strike on the larynx is very effective and painful. It affects the airway, the blood supply to the brain and bruises the thyroid gland causing severe pain and nausea.

If you bite the neck or throat, get your teeth into the thick muscled area to the sides. These areas have a good blood supply and bleed very quickly. Because of the myth that when the throat is cut it means instant death, this will probably cause your attacker to become frightened, especially as he has no way of viewing the damage. Remember: bite hard, rip and tear. Be ready to follow up with another attack.

How to punch . . .

Making a fist is not as simple as many people imagine; making a good fist in order to strike with strong impact is a technique in itself.

The fist should be clenched with the thumb resting under and outside the second bone of the index and middle finger, so clamping the index and middle fingers into a tight bunch. The fist should be tipped forward so that the back of the hand runs in a straight line with the back of the forearm.

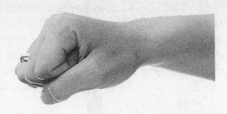

Making a fist

The two knuckles at the base of the index and middle fingers are the only parts of the hand that should make contact with a target when punching.

Any cocking or twisting of your wrist will cause an injury to it on impact. Any contact with the third and fourth knuckle may result in a broken hand.

The reason karate students do press-ups on their knuckles is to strengthen their wrists and to practise maintaining that straight line from the two knuckles to the elbow. This may be practised on carpet or thin gym mat without causing discomfort. Later you can move on to hitting a soft punch bag or a polystyrene pad.

If you want to be able to punch effectively and naturally, this will need to become a part of your daily training routine. These are just the basics of making a fist, to go further would be to enter the realms of martial arts.

Fighting on the ground

It is possible that during a struggle you may find yourself in the frightening situation of being on the ground while your opponent is still standing.

In the case of being attacked by only one man, roll on to your back and pull your knees up, so that your feet are off the ground pointing towards your attacker. Whichever way he moves, wriggle around and keep your feet pointed at him.

If he comes within range, kick at him in a cycling fashion. In this way if he grabs one foot, the other will kick him off. This is a very hard defence to penetrate. Keep your feet high aimed at his chest if he tries to dive on you, you will be able to take his weight

and throw him aside. With time consumed in attempting to get through this defence, combined with the noise you should continue to make, there is a very good chance that he'll give up.

When rising to your feet, keep your eyes on the attacker or in the direction in which you last saw him. If he returns to the attack before you gain your feet go back to your original position.

If you find yourself on the ground with more than one attacker, then resort to the methods described in Gang Attacks (see page 84). Get your head near to a fence or wall so that you can try to get to your feet with something protecting your back.

Try to get your feet under you and guard your head with your arms. Keep your eyes on your attackers and watch for your chance.

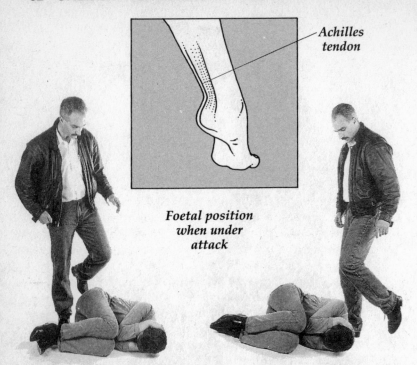

*Achilles
tendon*

***Foetal position
when under
attack***

When on the floor being kicked and unable to move because of the ferocity of the attack, curl up in the foetal position. Place your hands over the back of your head, with your elbows in front of your face and your knees pulled up touching your elbows. This way you have the maximum protection against any permanent damage. Keep thinking, do not panic and wait for the attack to subside. When it does, look for your opportunity to strike back.

There may be a situation where you end up holding a foot in your hand. Not much use holding a size ten shoe, you might think, but this is not so. Keep the foot off the ground so that he has to hop. Try to get to your feet. If you can, just pull him towards you and, as he hops, push him backwards. He will fall over, so you can then counter-attack or escape while he is on the ground. If you can't get up and you have hold of a foot, sink your teeth into the Achilles tendon just above the heel on the rear of the lower leg. Any damage to this will prevent him standing or walking, once again allowing you to escape.

Chapter Nine

STRATEGY FOR SURVIVAL

I have already emphasised the importance of an immediate and positive reaction to any violent assault. We have learned that this is as much to shock an attacker and unsettle his confidence (and thereby persuading him to back off) as it is to actually floor him. Although the two things are by no means mutually exclusive!

But what if, despite what you've read here, you panic? Perhaps he's holding a Stanley knife to your throat and your courage fails you. You hesitate and find yourself having to comply with his instructions. After all, we are all human. What do you do now? And how long do you wait?

During escape and evasion training in the SAS, if you are taken prisoner by the enemy you are taught to make your escape attempt as early as possible to overcome "the shock of capture". There are several sound reasons for this.

- The longer you leave it, the further you will be from familiar territory and known potential help.

- The more time that elapses, the easier it is for the enemy to secure you more effectively.

- The longer you wait, the weaker you become physically and mentally. Your fear can build up to a mind-numbing helplessness and hopelessness. (Shock of capture.)

- The longer you are held captive, the easier it is for your enemy to get the measure of you and to find your weaknesses, reinforcing his dominance by engendering even more fear in you.

All these points apply equally in a case of sexual assault when an attacker will want to get you to a place where he feels more secure.

So, if you get it wrong initially, stay cool.

Mentally regroup. Breathe deeply, slowly and steadily. Don't talk. Force yourself to think ahead. EVALUATE the situation.

Prepare to act as soon as an opportunity appears. There is always a tendency to wait for a better one. Don't, it will get harder not easier.

When you do act, the effect on your attacker will be almost as devastating as it would have been if you had reacted immediately. The sudden change in your demeanour from submissive victim to ferocious she-cat will still stun and disable him.

But it must be exactly that. A sudden change and not a visible build up to anger that will warn and prepare him. Keep your anger inside you and then explode suddenly.

It is likely to be your attacker's use of a weapon that will make you hesitate. But as his believed dominance over you increases, so will his confidence and the more confident he becomes the more mistakes he will make. He may put the knife in his pocket or away to the side. If he does, this is the time to go for it just as he begins to relax.

Don't attack while his weight is on you. Weight saps energy, so try to get yourself into a position where you are on equal ground, for example when you are both standing up facing one another. If he turns his back for a second and you cannot run, you have nothing to lose. **Attack! attack! attack!**

Having said this it is important to remind you of our first principle, fight back immediately. A man with a knife is expecting you to look at the weapon while he tells you about the danger you are in and hopes to dominate you with terror. He won't expect you to act without listening to him first.

Gang attacks

This is a nightmare scenario and probably the most difficult situation to deal with. When confronted by a group of men, it is imperative to know what their programming is and how to deal with it.

If you are attacked without warning, then you should dispatch your assailant as violently and effectively as possible using the techniques you have learned. When this is successful, the shock effect of seeing a pack member severely hurt will probably create a pause in activity long enough for you to escape from the situation.

If you are grabbed again or chased you must be prepared to continue your fight.

However, most such groups have a pack mentality. They follow the leader and need to build up to a pitch before actually commencing an assault. They do this to build up their own bravado and confidence, usually by laughing each other into a state of semi-hysteria, and goading each other on to commit greater acts of violence.

The final phase usually begins with a touch, which becomes a grope intended to provoke the woman to respond with some kind of weak and inadequate defence. This is the prompt for the men to grab and hold, or even to strike the woman, and eventually she will be beaten or pinned down and held helpless.

There is a predictable pattern here from both the men and intended female victim. As always, the best time to break the expected sequence is right at the beginning as you are being surrounded. Continue determinedly in your direction of travel, no matter how slowly. Try not to go around people and do not change course. The sight of a defenceless woman getting more and more frightened, changing direction and running in circles is just the stimulus required for the next stage to occur.

February 1993, Southport, Merseyside
A gang of six men attacked a fifteen-year-old girl and frog-marched her fifty yards to an unmanned railway station. Five of them held her down while the other one raped her.

She was so traumatised that it was seventeen days before she could bring herself to tell her mother, who then called in the police.

Do not attack yet as you haven't been assaulted, but prepare yourself by identifying the ringleader. Inevitably he will be the biggest or the one doing most of the talking. He is your best target. He will probably come closest to you and is most likely to touch you first. Deal with him and you deal with the group.

MAKE EYE CONTACT WITH HIM AND HOLD IT.

Use your confidence to firmly request him to move out of your way, all the time continuing to move forward.

Face him down. If he breaks eye contact, move forward and out of the group.

If he continues to block your way, close the distance without making actual contact and hold the eye contact.

There is a chance at this stage that he will laugh, "do you a favour" and let you pass. However it doesn't *always* work like that.

Should you be unable to pass through the group, try to prevent an attack from behind you by getting something solid at your back, such as a fence or wall. This will allow you to see everything that is happening and will prevent the pack from pulling you down from behind. It takes far more courage to attack someone from the front.

Do not allow minor touches from the rear to distract you. Maintain eye contact with the leader and direct all your responses to him alone. Ignore the others and they will gradually quieten and watch.

Begin to get angry inside.
Consider your first attacking move and be ready to use it on the first man that grabs you.
Try not to be drawn by a slight touch – this will be used to gauge your reaction and to see if you have any concealed weapons.
Do not get involved in meaningless conversation. Insults and talk are just a way of reading your body language and breaking down your confidence.
Maintain your silence. This again is unexpected and disconcerting to them. Coil your anger up inside like a spring and wait for the attack.

By not providing the expected responses they may well decide that you "are no fun" and leave for better sport elsewhere. If they decide to do this, allow them to leave and say nothing. Do not respond to apologies or friendly gestures. Maintain your position and be aware that their change in attitude may be a deception.

If an attack comes, carry out the most violent and painful attack you can remember – immediately and whole-heartedly. Then move past the injured attacker and out of the circle to escape.

At this stage their first reaction may well be to care for their wounded friend before they come looking for revenge.

Should you be unable to get help or make an escape, begin the sequence again by getting your back to a wall. But think of an alternative weapon or technique. They will be more prepared the second time around.

If you had a weapon in your right hand, then transfer it to your left and conceal it from view. Remember, never show your attacker a weapon. The first he should know of its existence is when it hits him.

Indicate that you still have it in the original hand. Use anything that may give you the element of surprise. Look wild and insane and mumble incoherently; many people have an irrational fear of "mad" people because they are unpredictable. This ploy can help to unsettle your attacker's programming. Keep thinking and looking for the new leader, then go at him again.

Once you have begun an attack on a particular person or target, make your aim an *obsession*. No matter what happens, force through your attack and don't let anything stop you short of unconsciousness. This display of determination will be tremendously unnerving to your attackers.

Even if they beat you down, the fun will have gone out of the game. You didn't play by the rules, you spoiled it. With the change in atmosphere, the chance of rape will be reduced. Remember:

- **Maintain eye contact.**
- **Don't be deflected from your path.**
- **Don't converse except to give orders.**
- **Protect your back.**
- **Attack and go through the group.**

Dressed to kill

This well-known expression is all too appropriate in the context of this subject. Women like to look sexy and attractive and men like to look at women who are sexy and attractive – it's the natural way of things. But it can also trigger unwanted attention from the very people you wish to avoid.

As part of your everyday strategy for survival, it is wise to remember another expression: there is a time and a place for everything. Many women become irritated when advised that they shouldn't wear "provocative" clothes whenever they choose. Their annoyance is understandable but there are nevertheless certain sensible precautions they should take to avoid the problems that looking good can cause – however unfair that may seem.

Like it or not, a well-groomed and attractively dressed woman is a more likely attack target. And that can apply to a stylish business suit as well as a chic little cocktail dress. An attacker will want to hurt you just because you walk so well, because you look good and because he thinks that you wouldn't give the likes of him the time of day. He will convince himself that you are a "cocky stuck-up bitch, who is just asking for it".

Naturally, if you can always arrange to be accompanied by a friend when going out for the evening most problems will be avoided (provided, of course, it is a friend). I recognise this isn't always possible, and here are some guidelines that will help you to protect yourself from an attack.

Wear flat shoes when walking to and from an event. Take your high heels with you and change as you arrive. You can run a hell of a lot faster, keep your balance and fight far more effectively with flat shoes on.

Wear a long coat as this protects you from provoking the response previously mentioned and can provide considerable protection in the event of an attack taking place. The length protects your knees, the thickness provides a defence against being stabbed and the collar will help to prevent you from being strangled.

Remove any pierced earrings until you arrive at and after you leave an event: earrings can be held by an attacker and painfully used to control your head movements. Put flashy rings in your purse and put your purse in your coat pocket, not inside your handbag. If your handbag is snatched, your money and credit cards are still safe with you.

By all means carry your handbag strapped across your body to prevent it being snatched in a busy street. But when alone, carry it over one shoulder so that it can be released easily. With your purse in your pocket it really isn't worth fighting for. If it is strapped across your body, a mugger may well assault you in order to get the bag free.

If you wear a hat, hold it in place with a hat pin. If you are threatened use the hat pin in the same way as a tail comb.

6th February 1991, Clapham, London

A judge called for a police investigation into the sound made by personal alarms for women after jailing a convicted rapist aged thirty-three, who had carried out another attack.

He said: "If these alarms are going to be effective, they must be distinguishable from car alarms. Then this girl might have been saved."

The attacker had gouged his victim's cheek with a screwdriver but failed to pull off her all-in-one jump suit.

He was jailed for seven years.

Safe and sound

Make a point of backing up your acoustic defences with a personal sound alarm. There are several makes on the market, but some do not produce the required effect. A sound alarm must be loud, reliable and simple to use.

The sound must be loud enough to hurt the ears in order to shock the attacker and to attract attention. The noise must not resemble a car alarm as everyone ignores that as a nuisance these days! It must not switch off without some difficulty, such as the replacement of a pin or the release of a locking cap.

It must be reliable as you only get one chance to use it. If it doesn't go off, it's too late.

It must also be small, simple and quick to use. Carry a sound alarm in your pocket or in your hand so it is readily available. It is no good rummaging around in your handbag when you need it.

A screech alarm (an aerosol can that emits a high-pitched sound) can also be a useful defence against obscene telephone callers. Simply fire the alarm down the mouthpiece when you receive a call. Then it's the caller who will have the problem, not you.

Some of the alarms available in the UK today (1992) that I have examined are*

Name	Advantages and Disadvantages	*Rating
Suzy Lamplugh Alarm	Aerosol type. Loud, simple, small. Locks on.	****
Walkeasy	Aerosol type. Loud, simple, small. Locks on. Has been known to stick on first go.	****
Chubb Personal Protector	Not loud enough. Pin release too small, easily muffled, batteries may run out. Sounds like a car alarm.	*
Bodyguard	Small clip-on type with pin release and lock on. Loud but gets muffled by clothing.	***
Shrill Alarm	Aerosol type. Loud, simple, small. Stops on release of pressure.	**

A sound alarm is only an aid to your protection. It may frighten off your attacker or summon help, but it is no guarantee to your safety and you must have your personal techniques for fighting back ready if it fails.

Sound alarms are available from many shops and DIY stores selling household security items.

At home alone

Although I hope you've come to learn and accept that the unthinkable can happen, there is no need for us to become paranoid about safety so that it spoils our quality of life.

It is far better to introduce a few personal safety rules into our daily routines and to make a point of keeping to them.

Here are a few pointers:

- Make sure your house or flat is secure and fitted with window locks.
- Do not leave easily accessible windows open at night.
- Always lock outside doors. If other people, such as previous tenants or old boyfriends, still have keys change the locks.

---

* Some alarms may have been improved since this date

- Draw your curtains after dark and if you think there is a prowler outside call 999.

- Don't put your first name in the phone book or by your doorbell as this will make it obvious that you are a woman living alone.

- If you see signs of a break-in at your home, do not enter. Call the police.

- If you are selling your home, don't show people around on your own. Let them make an appointment and leave a contact number, then ensure that your estate agent or a friend is present.

When out walking

- Don't take shortcuts through lonely areas, day or night.

- Walk facing the traffic so that no one can pull up behind you.

- If you go jogging or take a dog for a walk regularly, try to vary the time that you go and the route that you take.

- If a car stops and you are threatened, use your voice loudly and leave quickly. If you have high heels take them off to run.

- Carry a sound alarm.

- Don't flash expensive jewellery.

- If you are taken home at night by a friend or in a taxi ask the driver to watch you enter the house before departing.

- If someone grabs your bag, let it go. It isn't worth fighting for.

- If you think you are being followed, go to the nearest occupied area and call the police.

On public transport

- Avoid lonely bus stops.

- On an empty bus, sit downstairs in view of the driver or conductor.

- On a train, sit near the guard's compartment and avoid carriages without central walkways.

- Try to call taxi firms which provide female drivers on request. Many offer such a service without any problem whatsoever. If the first company that you call cannot help, then try another; better still find one *before* you go out and keep the number for future reference.

- Black cabs are an inherently safer bet than mini-cabs – use only reputable firms and avoid cowboy outfits who do not properly vet their drivers.

When driving

- Make sure your car is well fuelled and serviced.

- Plan your route.

- Make sure you have money for the phone.

- Let people know where you are going and your expected route and time of arrival.

- Don't pick up hitch-hikers, male or female.

- Keep your valuables in a locked boot and out of sight.

- Park in well-lit areas.

- Have your keys ready before you arrive at your car and carry them as taught.

- If you need to speak to someone from the car, only wind the window down a couple of inches and keep the doors locked.

- Use a steering lock. It's a useful weapon when not in use. Also, you'll always know that the car will be where you parked it.

- Carry a heavy torch in the glove compartment.

If you break down in your car there are certain guidelines you should follow.

If you are on a motorway park as close to a telephone box as possible. Call the breakdown services, return to your car and lock all doors. If you need to speak to someone from the car, only wind down the window a couple of inches. Refuse assistance from unofficial people. If you are in a town go to a garage or shop to call for assistance. If you are in the countryside late at night, park the car and walk to either the nearest phone box (if you know where the nearest one is located) or call at the nearest house and ask them to phone for assistance. Return to your car, lock all the doors and windows and wait for assistance. Only enter the house if a female is present. If you do a lot of motoring it is advisable to join a motoring organisation such as the AA, RAC or National Breakdown.

Kidnap

If you are forced to drive a dangerous person to an unknown destination, remember that you have control because you are driving the vehicle. The faster you go, the more difficult it will be for the attacker to assault you without risking his own life. If he doesn't wear his seat belt he can be projected through the windscreen with one hard stamp on the brake pedal.

One option is to cause a crash when the car is travelling at a relatively slow speed. Choose a public area, but one where it will not endanger pedestrians. Bumping another car up the rear in a traffic queue would have the desired effect. The car will stop and the driver will get out to talk to you. Don't wait until he gets to the car – that is what your attacker is expecting. Go for it while he is trying to plan his response to the crash.

Stopping right next to a policeman or police station may well take some courage but imagine how your abductor will feel if you do. You have called his bluff – he can be charged for his relatively minor offences or go down for murder.

You will have put fear and uncertainty into his mind. He will be open to attack and you will be in a position to escape. Remember you aren't going on a picnic, he is taking you somewhere to attack you.

If you choose to crash into a stationary object, pick something that will give a little, like a car or a bush. Lamp posts and trees can be very unforgiving. You might kill yourself.

Be very aware of pedestrians, don't hurt an innocent bystander in your attempt to stop the car.

If you are forced to go anywhere against your will, whether by car or on foot, it is always best to act sooner rather than later. Take positive action and hence the initiative. Remember the further you are from occupied buildings, the more danger you are in. He is not going to change his mind.

February 1993, Salisbury, Wiltshire
After leaving a nightclub at 1.15 a.m. a twenty-two-year-old married woman passed two men in the shadows on her way home.

Following a brief exchange of words she continued walking, but the two men quickly caught up with her again.

While one man stayed behind the woman, the other stepped in front of her. He then grabbed her, ripped off her clothes, and raped her.

At the disco

If an incident occurs with your date involving a scuffle or threats being exchanged with another man, then it is always a wise precaution to leave before closing time. Otherwise the other party may be waiting outside for you.

A little tact can go a long way under these circumstances. Explaining that you wish to leave because you are frightened and want to avoid conflict will often draw the predictable male response from your date! He'll want to stay put to prove that he isn't afraid and is quite capable of looking after you.

So have a discreet word with the head doorman and explain the situation. Tell him you intend to leave and would appreciate it if he ensured that you weren't followed immediately. Then persuade your partner to leave for some other reason. You don't feel well or you have a headache. Or alternatively that you feel in very, very high spirits and want to go home *now*!

If you have to use a taxi, get it to come to the door of the venue and don't hang around outside waiting for it. Stay inside until it arrives.

Chapter Ten

DATE RAPE

This relatively new expression has arrived from the United States and has received much coverage in the press, especially concerning cases that involve well-known personalities.

It is worth including a small chapter here, not only because it is a common form of assault but because it can so often happen without malice aforethought and have sad consequences for both parties.

Such situations are particularly difficult to handle from your viewpoint because the man involved will be someone you know (and probably like) or someone you would like to know.

A woman might allow herself to be chatted up at a party by a seemingly charming and respectable fellow and in a wild moment accept an innocent invitation for coffee, only to find he transforms into a monster behind closed doors. Sure, that happens. But more likely is a misreading of each other's body language, words spoken and those little discreet signals that pass between the sexes. All these are interpreted against each party's mental database of past experiences – but what happened on one occasion won't necessarily happen in similar circumstances in the future.

Let me explain. The first sexual encounter in a man's youth was probably with a girl he needed to persuade and coax into having sex with him. He may have experienced rejection after rejection which eventually led to nervous compliance, with "No" becoming "Oh, all right then".

You may recognise your own voice here. Fine, it's all part of growing up.

Similarly, token resistance can frequently be a part of foreplay. A sort of ritual between new lovers. Fine again. But get it wrong and you can both be in serious trouble. So remember, it is important not to lead a man down the paths of his previous experience without knowing how far you intend to go.

Alcohol can also play a big part in an unfortunate turn of events. A drink too many may make a woman drop her guard or act more amorously then she intended. Likewise, too much alcohol can increase a man's bravado and frequently trigger aggression in someone who is usually quite amiable. Indeed it can be a very dangerous cocktail.

So watch the booze. If you're tempted to accept or to make an invitation to be somewhere alone, think twice. Isn't it wiser to get to know each other better when you are both a little more sober? Some men do not think with their heads once they are aroused! Be aware of this before any physical activity begins.

Coffee is the greatest aphrodisiac

For generations, sex has followed "Come up for coffee" more frequently than any other invitation. If you invite a man for coffee alone with you, or accept his invitation, you are putting yourself at risk. It is all part of the secret language of lovers that different people understand and interpret in different ways.

Should you take that risk, make it absolutely clear that you mean coffee and a chat *and nothing else*. Be firm, don't allow him to misconstrue your intentions in any way. But even after having done this there is a very good chance that he will agree with everything you say and not believe one word. So be warned.

If you do not want sex it is best not to make such invitations. A polite and cheerful excuse like an early start at the office the next day will not offend if he really likes you. And if you like him a lot make a date for your next meeting.

If you are not sure that you want sex say no and wait until you are absolutely certain. Confusion on your part can lead to a serious misunderstanding later. You are, of course, entitled to change your mind at any stage, but don't light the fuse yourself. It is always easier for a man to make you feel guilty for saying **"No"** if he can claim that you led him on earlier.

If you're enjoying a man's company but have no inclination to have sex with him, make your position about sex clear before any pestering begins – it isn't a taboo subject any more. Let him know you enjoy his company and want to talk – but nothing else. Remember flirting is sex, kissing is sex, and petting is sex. Try not to set off down the slope because it is always hard to stop once you have started.

Of course, this makes the assumption that you always *know* what you want! You may well decide that you do want to go home with a man and have sex, only to change your mind later when an ugly personality begins to shine through the smile.

If he is your regular boyfriend and he threatens to leave in a sulk, let him go. Don't make up on the doorstep with a kiss as that is just the cue to start again. Make up tomorrow.

If a man will not leave your house after persistent requests, don't show your anger. Stay calm and find an excuse to leave the room or the house, go to the phone and call a friend or in a more serious case (any time you are frightened) the police. If the man hasn't been violent he will probably just be cautioned and released. If he comes back, call the police again. Never warn such a person of your intentions if you have cause for concern, just do it. If the phone is in the same room as you both, pretend you've run out of milk – or whatever – and make an excuse to call on a neighbour or go outside and use a public phone box to call for help.

When someone is persistently frightening you to the point where you are unable to ask for help, phone one of the organisations at the end of this book and talk about your problem. They may be able to offer alternatives that you haven't considered.

Let us assume that despite your best efforts a situation is getting decidedly unpleasant. Perhaps you are alone with a man you have dated and he is laying a lot of guilt on you, indicating that he may become aggressive and claiming that you have led him on. Gradually you are being put in a position where your fear of his reaction if you say no is strong enough to persuade you that it may be best to comply.

But he hasn't yet assaulted you and therefore you would be wrong to attack him. As yet he is using only intimidation as a weapon, however unnerving that might be.

It is important in such a situation to continue to make it clear that you do not want him to continue. Maintain a physical distance between you. Just because you have been kissing earlier does not mean you have to now. A kiss will be seen as uncertainty on your part and will encourage further attempts. Do not forgive earlier bad behaviour and do not have the tables turned on you by starting to explain yourself.

The following advice may be completely alien to most women but it may get you out of trouble without either of you resorting to violence. There is nothing more unnatural to women than deliberately appearing repulsive or unattractive, but imagine the response of a man when he realises that his dream girl has a few unpleasant personal habits. Don't be too obvious or too sudden, but gradually introduce one or two unseemly characteristics.

If you can, slip into your kitchen and chew on a clove of garlic; absent-mindedly begin to pick your nose; scratch a bit; develop a hacking cough; hawk and make a show of spitting into your handkerchief or into an ashtray. Tell him that you've had this cough for weeks and it won't clear up. Casually drop in some foul language, as if you always talk like that when you know someone. Mention your periods. Tell him they smell strange. Tell him you have a strange vaginal discharge.

I think you may perceive a "cooling of his ardour".

Coping with rape

Rape is a very serious offence. In law it is considered second only to murder and kidnap. Despite the good advice given in this book, there is no guarantee that you will never be a victim.

Now, you may feel a man isn't qualified to give advice to women on coping with such a matter, but that is not quite true. Men can be and are raped by other men more commonly than you might think. A friend of mine committed suicide after being gang raped in Singapore in 1972.

No person can say they really know what it is like to be raped unless they have been a victim, but a man is just as capable of imagining the vile consequences and mental anguish that follows such an act. Some of these reactions will be exactly the same as yours, some even worse. The sense of shame at being abused and the shame of cowardice for having "let it happen" may be even stronger.

We have talked a lot in this book about mental programming and mental preparation in facing the unthinkable. I've little doubt that you feel far more confident now about your personal safety than you did when you started reading.

So try to imagine now how you might feel mentally as well as physically, if you ever did become a victim. Dwell on it, use your imagination. Consider it in the way that all of us do from time to time when we wonder how we would cope if we were blind, lost a limb or were diagnosed as having cancer. Not "Oh, I couldn't cope with that!" Rather "This is how I would have to cope." Think positive. **Be a survivor not a victim,** mentally as well as physically.

Rape is a deep and personal attack on anyone's dignity. It is utterly degrading and loathsome and can hurt those close to you as well as the victim. The physical effect of rape rarely causes permanent damage to the body. The main trauma is to the mind. So reprogramme yourself now, think clearly and positively along these lines:

If ever I am raped . . .

I will never, ever let the scumbag who did it have the satisfaction of ruining my life.

I WILL KNOW IT WAS NOT MY FAULT – Nothing I could do would ever justify an assault of this nature.

I will not feel guilt or shame over whatever action I did or did not take.

I am entitled to have submitted. No one has the right to dictate what I should have done in such circumstances.

I will not feel shame. I will not be afraid to cry and release my emotions and to share my feelings with a friend or counsellor.

I will remember that for every sick or evil man out there, there are thousands of good men.

I will be patient with my partner and understand that he is suffering too.

I will always be proud of myself and hold on to my dignity.

What else?

Fitness

The whole point of the techniques discussed in this book is that you do not need to be young or physically fit to use them. They will work for any person of any age and even people with disabilities. Like anything, though, it pays to be quick and alert and if you are physically fit you will probably have a greater chance to escape.

Realism in training

One problem with virtually all forms of self-defence training is lack of realism.

It is difficult to learn to dance without a teacher and it is difficult to learn any fighting technique without someone to correct faults or improve them.

As I have clearly stated, the fighting techniques and the attitudes that I encourage are dangerous weapons. They should *not* be practised on other persons without the supervision of an expert.

Practise them on contact pads or punch bags. Go through the techniques without weapons slowly with a friend just to be sure that you understand them.

DO NOT practise with improvised weapons on people and do not try to inject realism of any kind into your own personal training.

Should you wish to attend an Unleash the Lioness course then write to **Immediate Response Security Ltd, PO Box 391, Sutton, Surrey SM1 1TE.**

Chapter Eleven

THE LAW AND YOU

Can you imagine the uproar if a woman acting in self-defence against an attacker caused him such severe damage that she in turn was punished for her behaviour? Yes, I'm sure you can!

Strangely enough it is not completely out of the question under the laws of the United Kingdom. However, such cases are rare indeed. This country has a good police force, good barristers and good judges but you must be aware that there are *some* strange apples in the barrel who may be interested in proving a point rather than considering the circumstances fully.

So it is important to know exactly how the law views assault situations in order to protect yourself from going too far.

I took these problems to Mr Bill Bache of Pye-Smith, a Salisbury-based firm of solicitors. Mr Bache is H.M. Deputy Coroner for Wiltshire and has over twenty years' experience of criminal law; he has been described as having substantial experience in this field. His answers led me to conclude the following:

It is of paramount importance to understand in any self-defence situation that the potential victim must make every reasonable effort to avoid a conflict and to show that he or she does not wish to fight. If, of course, the first thing you see or feel is a blow or an arm across your throat then it is no longer reasonable to expect you to make this clear.

If you are being attacked, such that it is reasonable to believe your life is in danger, you may take proportionate retaliatory action against your assailant in order to prevent or stop a serious assault against yourself. You do not know at what point the attack will stop and so it may be reasonable to assume the worst.

When you are acting in defence of your life, it is within the law to use such force as is reasonable and necessary to stop someone from causing you injury or of depriving you of your liberty.

After the attack, you must be able to show or state why you

thought it was reasonable and necessary, but you are not by law required to grade your weight of response down to "a nicety". In other words, within broad limits you will not have to justify too precisely why one course of action which took place was preferable to a different possible action. You just did the first thing that came into your mind to save your life at the time. What you believed was taking place is as valid as what actually did take place. If the behaviour of the attacker caused you to fear for your life and this was your genuine concern, then it would be difficult to show that a high level of force was unreasonable or unnecessary.

If a man threatens you it is unwise to attack him even though you are frightened. However, if you believe that he is about to attack you it is a viable option to strike first. Likewise, if you are being threatened with violence and have no means of escape and you believe an attack is about to take place, you are within your legal rights to launch the initial attack in order to escape. In the case of Woodward and Koessler 1958, it was held that "Injury includes intimidation of a sort which is capable of producing injury through the operation of shock."

The court's interpretation of what is reasonable will also depend on who your attacker is. If it is another female or a twelve-year-old boy, and not a grown man, they may decide an action that would have been acceptable against a large man is not reasonable in these circumstances. Neither is it reasonable to continue to attack someone once they are no longer capable of assaulting you, or if they are in the act of departing from the scene. So, once you have gouged his eye, bitten off his nipple, and stuck your keys in his chest and he is lying on the floor bleeding, it is not reasonable to kick him in the head. But you may use reasonable force to restrain him if in your opinion he has committed an arrestable offence.

Remember, if you believe your life is in danger and that you would have been violently assaulted, the court will sympathise with you and your actions even if your attacker says later that he "was only joking", providing that he gave you good cause at that time to believe otherwise.

As you can see there are many grey areas in self-defence. You must be sure that you are actually being assaulted or threatened in such a way as to make you fear for your safety. You must look for the opportunity to avoid a conflict by moving away, responding calmly to verbal abuse or by summoning help.

Just because you are at a bus stop at night alone with a stranger and he taps you on the shoulder, does not constitute assault. He may want a light or to ask the time. If you struck him under these circumstances you would be at fault and could expect to be subject to criminal proceedings. It is safest to let hot air blow cold and wait and if an assault begins to take place or if you are being attacked or restrained against your will, you must fight back.

Offensive weapons

It is illegal to go anywhere armed. This means to carry an item that has no other purpose than to be used to injure, such as knuckle-duster, a flick-knife, Mace spray, etc, or with the "specific" intention of using something as a weapon. If you are found in possession of items such as these you are committing an arrestable offence. The onus is on you to show that you have lawful authority or reasonable excuse for being in possession of such an item. If you use items such as these in your own defence, you may still have to answer charges for being in possession of them later.

It is an offence to carry any object with the "specific" intention of using it as a weapon. However, if you happen to have an everyday item that you have a legitimate reason for possessing at the time an assault takes place (such as car keys or a comb) it is not an offence to have it about your person. What you do with it must still be reasonable and necessary.

If a person deliberately put herself in a position to be attacked or provokes an attack, she could be considered to be inciting or provoking an incident and would be at fault.

It would be illegal and extremely foolish to try any of the techniques in this book without having just cause.

If an everyday object has been altered so as to make it effective as a weapon (such as sharpening the tail of a comb) this will be construed as carrying a weapon and as such is also an offence.

The Police

At the time of writing, the officer with responsibility for advice on personal safety at the Metropolitan Police in London is

Inspector Shirley Tulloch.

She is a strong believer in what has come to be known as the Bash-and-Dash tactic of self-defence – striking back as fiercely as you can in order to escape an assault.

"A woman is justified in fighting back," she has said. "You have to defend yourself with everyday items. If a woman caused injury, serious injury, by jabbing her keys into someone's eyes, she would be justified if she was fighting for her life, if it was a case of him or her. But there is no way we would recommend women to carry actual weapons."

March 1993, Wakefield, West Yorkshire
A man who bit off a chunk of another man's nose walked free from the Crown Court after a jury decided he had acted in self-defence.

George Boyle, now retired as a Superintendent with the Metropolitan Police after thirty-five years' service, was able to talk freely about police attitudes to intended assault victims who fight back.

When I pointed out that many women hesitated to counter-attack effectively, even viciously, because they feared prosecution, he replied, "It would be a particularly poor policeman who attempted to arrest a woman who had been attacked by a man. However, there have been cases of women against women, and men against men, where all parties had been charged. But those were different circumstances to those under discussion."

He had never, in all his years with the Met, come across a situation where a woman had been charged for injuring her assailant.

I asked what advice he would give to a woman who was worried about being arrested for hurting a man who was attacking her. He replied, **"Don't even consider it. Defend yourself if you are being attacked."**

He believes that the increase in violent crime over the last forty years is the most notable change in our society. He considers that attacks on women, including rape, should be thought of as violent crime statistics rather than classed separately as sex crime. Violent crime in general is escalating. Rape and mugging are really a part of this larger picture. In his experience rapists come from all walks of life, rich and poor, of limited and high intelligence. But in general violent people tended to be social inadequates who lean towards the lower end of the IQ scale. Violence to them is a way of coping with mental processes that are beyond their comprehension. When they run out of words they hit something or someone instead.

When asked if there was any advice he would give to women under attack. He answered:

Women should always fight back and defend themselves. If they scream, they should scream the word "Rape!" It is much more likely to attract attention and make people react.

A woman under attack should not swear abusively as people in hearing range might think that they are just another pair of rough necks who have been drinking too much.

George didn't believe that police advisers were restricted in what they could teach the public about self-defence. However, he felt that in reality teachers had simply not given it enough thought. Most trained fighters had difficulty putting themselves in the position of a frightened woman or of understanding how they would react in a potentially violent and life-threatening situation.

He cited one case where the rapist snatched his victims on a footpath and threw them into the hedgerow. The attack would come from behind in the dark. The first thing the victim would know was that she had been struck, the wind had been knocked out of her and she was lying on her back – trying to make sense of the situation with a masked man on top of her! If she didn't have a prepared plan in her head at this stage then she might never recover from the initial shock.

Where weapons are concerned he reaffirmed that people should not carry weapons as this is an offence. However, he knew of many cases where women had defended themselves with high-heel stiletto shoes to very good effect and that steel tail combs were a favourite weapon with prostitutes. "When it comes down to survival you use whatever you have to stay alive. Don't even consider it. Defend yourself if you are being attacked."

Useful addresses and telephone numbers

Rape crisis centres:

London   071 837 1600
Manchester   061 834 8784
Edinburgh   031 556 9437
Cardiff   0222 373 181
Birmingham   021 766 5366
Belfast   0232 249 696

Samaritans   Available nationwide 24 hours per day from your local telephone directory or directory enquiries.

Suzy Lamplugh Trust
            14 East Sheen Avenue, London SW14 8AS
            Tel: 081 876 1838

Metropolitan Police, Personal Defence Department
            Room 934, New Scotland Yard, London SW1H 0BG
            Tel: 071 230 1212

"I sincerely hope that you never have cause to unleash the lioness, but it's nice to know she's there just in case."

Robin Houseman